The Bite
of the Print

Frank and Dorothy Getlein

The Bite
of the Print

Satire and Irony in Woodcuts,
Engravings, Etchings, Lithographs
and Serigraphs

 Clarkson N. Potter Inc. / Publisher   *New York*

Published by Clarkson N. Potter, Inc., 1963, New York
Library of Congress Catalog Card Number 62-19294
Manufactured in Italy by Tipografia Toso, Torino

To our children,
Christine, Steve, Mary, Bill and Karl
With love

Acknowledgments

Our deep thanks to all who have produced, collected and written about prints.

Our special thanks to:

Lessing J. Rosenwald, whose own love and study of prints have contributed to the understanding and appreciation of them in America and elsewhere and whose own collection, from which most of the examples in this book are taken, is his gift to the nation; Elizabeth Mongan, former Curator, and Katharine Shepard, Assistant Curator, Graphic Arts, The National Gallery of Art.

FRANK AND DOROTHY GETLEIN

Table of contents

Index of plates

Chapter One
The Bite

The Bite

The prints most familiar to most people are those we all carry around on the ends of our fingers. These intricate little arrangements of loops and whorls and parallel curving lines have several points of similarity with prints as works of art. The clearest common point is the multiple image, or, as printmakers and curators, collectors and dealers quite properly insist, the multiple original. We go through our days touching, holding, feeling, hefting, pushing, pulling, and on everything we touch – wood, stone, paper, metal – we leave our prints. The housekeeper's despair, the policeman's hope, the prints are our mark. We have been there. The prints identify us. No matter how many prints we leave behind us, each is an original; each corresponds to all the others and it is that correspondence that is crucial, not the correspondence to the fleshy pads at our fingers' ends. For although we call those pads our prints, surely nothing is a print until it has been printed. The true fingerprint is the mark on the paper, made, like all prints, under pressure, and made, like many, by a rolling pressure. Even in criminal identification the print on the pistol is compared, not to the pad of flesh, but to the witnessed and certified mark that pad is known to make upon paper.

The same with the art print. The prints exist on paper, and they don't exist until they have been printed on paper. Each is an original. These are not printed so easily as fingerprints, but they can be printed in great numbers, many more than are contained in the usual edition of a print. Editions of prints are kept few in number for the same reason that fingerprints are, namely, for the profit of the printmaker.

It is clear enough why the enterprising burglar should restrict his print to as few as possible. For the print artist to do so too would seem to be something of a contradiction in terms. Part of the point of prints is that they come in large numbers. The more the merrier, one might think. The larger the edition, the greater the profit to both artist and public. Such indeed were the theory and practice of printmaking up until the last years of the nineteenth century. In those years a fundamental change took place in the relationship between paintings and prints, and the change is still in effect.

From the first prints of the fifteenth century one function of printmaking has been to supply paintings for everyman, and that function has assumed many different forms through the centuries. Right from the first the most direct expression of that function took place in prints that were frank copies of paintings. Many of the refinements of techniques and methods came into use because they permitted a closer equivalent in print of the effects of painting. On the other hand, most of the basic processes from etching and lithography to the serigraph were developed in the interests of speed and economy. What happened in the closing years of the nineteenth century was the application of the final quality of

1.
ANONYMOUS GERMAN (Ulm),
The Emperor and the Pope.
Woodcut, 1469-1473.

paintings to prints, an application that took place at first strictly in the marketing of prints. That final quality is rarity. Part – in some cases most – of the money value of a painting arises from the fact that there is only one. Despite the dedication of the print to the opposite principle, rarity was introduced into printmaking more or less in imitation of the market for old and genuinely rare prints. Certain prints of Rembrandt and Dürer command prices into the thousands of dollars chiefly because they are rare. This market fact being observed, the contemporary printmaker starting at the end of the last century was able to raise his own prices by limiting the number of impressions available. What for Rembrandt and Dürer was accomplished by time and the ills of fortune, the new printmaker could accomplish for himself by printing only a limited edition and then destroying the plate, stone, or block from which the impressions were printed. Once more the pleasures of the poor had been successfully stolen for the rich.

The most interesting connection, however, between fingerprints and art prints is their mutual association with the shady side of things, of life and society, human institutions and the human mind. Considered in itself, the fingerprint is a remarkable evidence of the ingenuity with which the universe is put together. Millions of men walk the earth and millions more have walked it in times past. Each is endowed with a set of these marks on the ends of his fingers; all are basically alike, yet no two are identical. Further, the fingerprint is the outward sign of man's individuality, that precious thing so desperately sought, so painfully achieved, so proudly proclaimed. The prisoner of the city or the suburb, deep in the fell clutch of punch cards or of lawn-tending, can stand erect, press his thumb to paper, and say of his mark, "It is my own, it is myself." The fingerprint, surely, merits our admiration and gratitude, deserves to be enshrined in the heart along with memories of childhood and hopes of heaven, but, curiously enough, this enshrining has not taken place, nor is it scheduled in the near future. The fingerprint takes its station in our society and in our psyches, not from its intricacy or individuality, but from the smudge it makes on white paper. The existence of the fingerprint became known through the art and science of criminal detection. The fingerprint remains an adjunct of the field of crime. The fingermarks most often printed are from hands raised against law and order.

The printmaker, too, seems to have his hand raised against society. From the beginning of European printmaking in the fifteenth century until the present, the printmaker, in his work, has looked askance and looked askew at all the powers that govern man, at Church and State, at science and art, at justice and war, at love itself. Among the earliest of prints were those celebrating the

2.
WILLIAM HOGARTH, 1697-1764,
The Laughing Audience,
(*The Author's Benefit*).
Engraving, 1733.

Dance of Death, and, one and all, those printmakers of five hundred years ago went out of their way to stress that the rulers of society, popes and princes, were prominent among those carried off by Death and, owing to their distinctive garb, equally prominent residents of Hell. These disrespectful pictures were created just as the art of portraiture was perfecting itself and oil painting was creating new and more glamorous images of these same princes and pontiffs. Portraiture continued, undeterred by the voices of gloom and doom in the print room; in the eighteenth century in England, in the hands of such practitioners as Sir Joshua Reynolds, the portrait in oil became a hymn, a lofty halleluiah, to the virtues of wealth; at the same time in the same place the engraver William Hogarth was cutting in metal the lines of the seamy side of the new heaven and showing beyond dispute that the rich, like the rest of us, are clods at heart.

In France, for a moment at the end of Hogarth's century, it looked as if the principles of the print – such as they are – had conquered in both art and life. The corrupt French court was dead or in jail, and the corrupt French painting that had pandered to that court was gone; Boucher, king of the boudoir, was dead and his closest rival, Fragonard, died broke in the brave new world with neither court nor courtly vices. Painter of the hour was Jacques Louis David. A revolutionist himself, David painted scenes in praise of ancient Rome for the edification of the new republic. The republic, of course, didn't last. It became a dictatorship, a terror, a directorate, a consulate, and so, by tiny changes, an empire. Napoleon revealed to the French *la gloire*, hidden for two centuries by the grandeur of Louis XIV and the sporting life of Louis XV and Louis XVI. As with Francis I and Cardinal Richelieu, *la gloire* seemed to consist chiefly in French armies overrunning all the other countries of Europe. While all this was going on, where, one may ask, was David, the painter of republican virtue? At the side, in spirit at least, of the emperor, doing his bit for tyranny, conquest, and slaughter. The austere paintings of Roman probity were succeeded by equally austere paintings of Napoleonic triumph. The revolutionary artist-moralist became a court painter without a moment's thought. *La gloire* became a matter of stagecraft in David's Napoleonic *tableaux vivants*, their chief use nowadays being to advertise French brandy, which, after all, has a glory of its own.

In Spain, of all places, however, *la gloire* ran into opposition and it came from the most unlikely source, an established court painter well into middle age. Francisco de Goya had collaborated with absolutism all his life. From an early age he had, indeed, scrambled to attain the favour and patronage of the absolutists. Having attained it, he designed tapestries for their palaces and painted portraits of their faces and figures. But under the pressure of the

Para eso habeis nacido.

3.
FRANCISCO GOYA, 1746-1828,
Los Desastres de la Guerra
(plate 12): *Is this what you were born for?*
Etching, aquatint, pub. 1863.

French invasion Goya produced one of the enduring monuments of the human spirit, a series of etchings called *The Disasters of War*. In these eighty-three prints the court painter became an eyewitness to history. He testified eloquently that the making of history requires the breaking of bones and brains. He raised the serious question of whether the history is worth the bones it breaks, a question that has influenced everyone's thoughts about war ever since. He made his testimony and raised his question in the form of prints.

Instances multiply as you move forward or backward in time, east or west on the surface of the earth. It is the aim of this book to multiply the instances, to show that a highly critical attitude toward man and society came into being with the making of the first prints in Europe and has remained a central part of printmaking in Europe and America ever since.

This critical attitude is neither "literary" nor "cerebral," nor any derogatory adjective chosen to imply: "Insofar as a work of art relates to human life, depicting that life or commenting upon it, just so far does the work fail as art." The great printmakers, it might as well be admitted at once, from the Germans who preceded Dürer, to Picasso in his most recent bullfight series, have one and all been concerned with the human life of which they have been part. In the first place they were all born decades and in some cases centuries before 1955, the year in which it was discovered that if you can tell what it is it isn't much good; besides the distressing ex post facto aspect of applying the new law to artists who never heard of it, there remains some doubt as to whether the law can be applied to prints as rigorously as it has been applied to paintings. Secondly, printmaking has always had that intense interest in materials and processes for which, under the new law, all things may be forgiven, even intelligibility. The printmaker's interest in his materials and methods stems from the fact that they are rather unusual materials and methods for picture making. For one thing, the methods all work backwards; a line intended for the left side of the final image must be drawn on the right side of the material on which the artist actually works. The well-known zinc lithograph of Dr. Gachet by Van Gogh looks more natural in the mirror than it does in the print itself; and occasionally in a lithograph by Daumier one or two letters appear reversed; the inexperience of Van Gogh and the haste of Daumier are both thus permanently recorded.

In any art form the limitations and specific potentials of the materials and methods have some part in shaping the image that the art projects. In sculpture there is a substantial difference between both of those and pieces put together by the welder's iron. It is a commonplace of histories that a fundamental change took place when sound was added to sight. The sonnet shapes and

4.
VINCENT VAN GOGH, 1853-1890,
Dr. Gachet.
Etching, 1890.

controls poetic thought to a degree that only rarely happens in free verse.

The print is no different. There is a clear connection between the methods of printmaking, particularly the classic methods – woodcut, engraving, and etching – and the general image the print creates. The print image in its widest sense, not only the picture or arrangement of lines and tones, but also and especially the mood, the social or psychological comment, the state of mind revealed or appealed to, the print image so understood reflects closely the print methods. Psychological and even philosophical questions arise: Do the methods create the effect, or does the effect, pre-existent, somehow, in the mind of the artist, choose the method? Take your choice. There are few maps and few theories of art that don't have some glimmer of truth in them, however fancifully the elaboration of truth has been pursued. The connection itself is inescapable. The very language bears witness to it. *Cut* is the basic action in preparing a block of wood to print a picture, and the word has become the generic name for an illustration; "cut" is also an insult or a snub, even a wound, and the body of prints from the fifteenth century until today is full of insults, snubs and wounds inflicted visually and deliberately. The etcher's tool is the *needle* and we needle a person by speaking of his imperfections or by challenging him to some feat we doubt he can do; etchings are full of such challenges and such persistent accounts of human imperfection. The *acid* used by the etcher also describes a state of mind, "sharp, biting, acrimonius," and the words apply to many of the most effective etchings ever made, and to the intelligence that made them. *Mordant* is the specific name for etcher's acid and *mordant* again is a type of intellect and a point of view, biting, sarcastic, caustic, often found in prints. *Bite* itself, which Webster keeps falling back on for the cast of mind and kind of comment here described, is also the technical term for the controlled corrosion of metal by acid which is the heart of the etching process.

Two characteristics are common to all prints. One is the reverse view mentioned earlier. The printman draws the reverse of what he prints. He acquires the habit of aiming in just the opposite direction from where he's looking, like Annie Oakley using a mirror to shoot over her shoulder. Miss Oakley was a virtuoso and virtuosity has always been a danger for printmakers. In the golden days when Edward VII was Prince of Wales and young ladies were invited to inspect the etchings of older gentlemen, it was the virtuosity – of the etchings – that was on exhibition, as it was that virtuosity the artist had in mind when he created the print and the collector when he bought it. Today virtuosity more often shows up in the textural embellishments the artist can think of and manage to incorporate in his plate. But the printmaker and

5.

KÄTHE KOLLWITZ, 1867-1945,
Weavers Cycle: Poverty.
Lithograph, 1897.

6.

OTTO DIX, b. 1891,
Lens Bombed.
Etching, 1924.

his public who accept the printed image of wire mesh and old bottle caps soldered into copper plate as the supreme achievement of prints are no less deceived than their grandfathers were in their adulation of plate-edges and the burr of a drypoint line attached to a perfectly ordinary scenic view. Virtuosity is always a danger. If the printmaker has the character to surmount that temptation, the discipline of working in reverse is helpful in several ways. It endows the artist with a moment of surprise when he actually prints his print. It keeps his mind closely on the immediate work before him. But above all this reverse vision forced upon the print artist also enforces a certain detachment, both from the work and from what the work is about, and detachment is the soul of the intellectual vision peculiar to the art of the print.

Does such enforced detachment occur in other forms of art? It does indeed. In the writing of dramatic comedy, for example, the necessity to build to a key line or to a key scene sometimes imposes a somewhat similar discipline upon the comic writer: he works backwards, from where he wants to get toward where he has to start from. Painting has been steadily losing this detachment imposed by the means. Direct painting, as practiced by the Impressionists and Post-Impressionists, led the way to a manner of painting ever more direct, with the artist necessarily ever less detached from his work. Painting in the mid-twentieth century, with its great emphasis on directness, has raised the value of the artist's sincerity to an all-time high, both aesthetically and financially. But that kind of artistic sincerity has never been present in printmakers, from the very nature of their work. They work in reverse; they create obliquely; their processes of production stand always at one or more removes from their product.

Pressure is the other thing all prints have in common. The pressure can vary from that exerted by a heavy, motor-driven press to that imposed by a spoonlike tool – or a spoon, for that matter – driven only by the hand. But wherever there is a print there has been pressure and in part the print is the record of pressure applied. The application of pressure and the state of being under pressure are both useful terms for describing the subjects of many prints as well as the attitude toward them taken by the printmaker.

Chapter Two

The Bitten

The Bitten

When you go past the general conditions under which all prints are created and examine the methods of particular kinds of prints, the relationship still holds between those methods and the visions of man they are used to create. In five centuries' time print methods have not changed, but they have been added to. The methods used in the fifteenth century for the first prints in Germany and Italy are still in use today, but there are new ones, both variations on the old, like aquatint and mezzotint, and truly new methods, notably lithographs and serigraphs, or silk-screen prints. Silk-screen came into use as an art medium in the year 1938 as a result of experiments in the W.P.A. art project. Silk-screen is by no means the youngest of the print processes, for the energy it released and the example it set have kept young American printmakers experimenting ever since. But silk-screen is certainly the youngest print process with any considerable body of work produced by a wide variety of artists. Silk-screen prints are not yet recognized as art by all print curators or all collectors of prints. The National Academy of Design, for example, as a matter of policy excludes serigraphs from Academy print shows. The Academy show, of course, has had the embarrassing experience of having to throw out a serigraph already accepted by its jury under the illusion that the print had been produced by some older process. Most objections to silk-screen come from its widespread commercial use, both in advertising and in reproductions of paintings.

Now all except the very latest print methods were historically developed or at least heavily exploited commercially at one time or another. At first, therefore, this institutional aversion to serigraphy seems a rather silly snobbism, like the gulf fixed in France between the royal and the imperial aristocracies, or the American social order based on the date of immigration.

Yet there really is a factual base for this snobbism or suspicion of the silk-screen print and it has nothing to do with the extreme youth of silk-screen or with the company it has kept, namely, advertising men and interior decorators. A very similar situation exists in the movies. Any movie critic worth his dour reputation will tell you that while the movies have to a large extent broken the sound barrier – that is, learned how to make good movies even with a sound track – film art has not yet recovered from the blows dealt it by Technicolor and by the wide screen. Visual effects are too easy and too spectacular; they are therefore dwelt upon lovingly to the detriment of emotional, intellectual and story effects. So in serigraphy. The silk-screen process makes color prints more easily, more inexpensively and with more immediate splashy impact than any other print method. The silk-screen process also lends itself to large-size prints, which have been relatively rare in print history. In short, everything about the

7.
ROBERT GWATHMEY, b. 1903,
Across the Field.
Color serigraph, 1944.

serigraph has cooperated to change prints from art objects collected in portfolios to art objects framed and hung upon the wall. Occupying thus the position of painting but, because of price and other factors, having nothing at all like the prestige of painting, serigraphs have become the decorator's best friend, a very dangerous position for any form of work aspiring to be an art. Prints are placed in interiors as if they were cushions or curiosities, to give a spot of color or to tickle a visitor's fancy. There even are silk-screen artists who will deliver the same print in a variety of colors, depending on the drapes, rugs and upholstery, just as, two generations ago, the culturally ambitious housewife could obtain engravings of *Sir Galahad, Homer Singing,* and *The Love-Lorn Shepherd,* in either sepia or green, depending on her own temperament.

Having faced these idols of the marketplace, we may observe that their worship is by no means universal among serigraphers, that the idols were certainly not set up in the first place by silk-screen men and that, in fact, a considerable number of high-quality serigraphs have been created in the brief history of the medium. Having so observed we may proceed to the methods by which silk-screen prints are made.

Silk-screen printing is the exception to the rule about printmakers working backwards, making their designs in reverse from the image that will appear in the final prints. The serigrapher works frontward. The design as it comes from his hand is the same shape and in the same direction as the design in the finished print. On the other hand, his creation of the design, at least in the original serigraph process, is negative. Like the woodcut artist, the silk-screen man actually works the areas which will not be printed. The design comes through on the paper from the areas on the screen which he has left alone.

Silk-screen is a stencil process. In the fundamental stencil process, such as is used in shipping rooms, for example, the design to be printed is simply cut out of some flat substance — cardboard, metal, celluloid, even sturdy paper is used. This stencil is laid on the surface to be printed; a brush loaded with ink is passed over the stencil; the stencil is lifted from the surface; the design appears on that surface. Silk-screen printing is simply a great refinement of that shipping-room commonplace. A fine silk — or nylon or even metal — screen is stretched across a frame of wood. Those parts of the area not to be printed are brushed with varnish and thus stopped-out. Ink, or lacquer, or oil paint is then forced through the open screen with a squeegee, a rubber blade mounted in a wooden holder wide enough to cover the entire screen on one pass. The color, being forced through, is deposited on the paper placed beneath the screen. The number of screens used on a single print can be multiplied indefinitely

8.

HONORÉ DAUMIER, 1808-1879,
*The Blue Stockings:
Pardon Me, Sir, if I
Disturb You a Little.*
Lithograph, 1844.

9.
Lithograph stone and printing press

and thus a wide range of colors can be employed. The screens themselves are easily restored to their pristine purity and may be used again and again. In the initial, or W.P.A. period of serigraphy, it was not uncommon for the identical screen to be used for all the colors in a print; the screen was simply washed out and redesigned between color runs on an edition of prints.

Variations have developed in silk-screen practice. Some artists draw their design on the screen with tusche, the crayon used in lithography. The whole screen is then stopped-out with glue or shellac; when this hardens, the tusche is washed out with kerosene or turpentine, leaving the stop-out material in place. Actual stencils of various materials are also applied to the screen. Because of its ease with color, serigraphy is often used in combination with other print methods — for example, to produce color areas in black line engravings or etchings. Ignoring the medium's easy way with color, a few silk-screen artists have successfully limited their work to black and white and produced very strong results. Other artists have experimented with the screen, the stencil, the papers and the color in order to give their work that quality of "hardness" that characterizes almost all the older print methods.

The next youngest print method, lithography, faced in its time the same scorn of practitioners of older methods and the same internal problem of finding a character for itself. The scorn has completely vanished and the internal problem has been solved in great part by the arrival of photo-mechanical processes to relieve lithography of its former commercial associations. Yet as we contemplate with satisfaction the lithograph's occupying the same pure, noncommercial milieu as we ourselves, we should keep in mind a number of historical facts. Lithography was discovered and initially exploited for strictly commercial motives. Its single greatest artist — Honoré Daumier — produced almost all his vast body of work as an artist-journalist doing a daily stint for *Charivari* as a kind of political-social commentator. The great growth of color lithography in the last decade or so derives from the commercial experiments of Toulouse-Lautrec in creating advertisements for music halls, night clubs and other low resorts.

Lithography is known as the "surface method" of printmaking for reasons which will be clear when the older methods are examined. Lithography, or polyautography, as it was called for some years, was accidentally discovered in 1796 by a Bavarian, Alois Senefelder. The inventor was not a graphic artist or an artist at all. He wasn't even, at bottom, a printer looking for a cheap and easy way to print. Senefelder, like his father before him, was a strolling player. He began writing plays, became convinced of his dramatic merit, and found his conviction shared by no one else, least of all the publishers of dramatic literature. To get his

10.

WOODCUT.

Block of *Countenance* by
James Van Dyk, in progress, 1961;
sharpening stones, knives, gauges,
spoons, Mars black, roller.

11.

ERNST BARLACH, 1870-1938,
God over the City.
Woodcut, 1921.

12.

EUGENE MECIKALSKI,
Moment of Impact.
Color wood engraving, 1958.

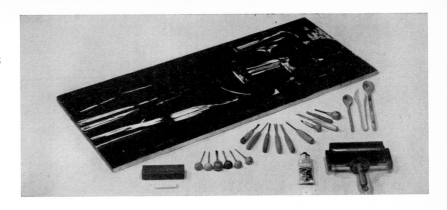

plays read and circulated, Senefelder determined to print them himself and to do so began experimenting with a cheap method of engraving or etching upon stone. He succeeded to the point of making some money by printing music, but his method of stone etching was never subject to complete control. In the course of trying to control it, the ambitious playwright discovered lithography.

The basic principle is that oil and water don't mix. The basic condition, making possible both Senefelder's discovery and the course of lithography ever since, is that Bavarian limestone absorbs water and oil with equal sympathy. After a slab of the stone has been ground smooth, the artist draws upon it with greasy crayon and then his design is fixed chemically in the surface of the stone. The stone is moistened; water is absorbed into all parts not drawn upon. The stone is inked; ink adheres only to the greasy parts and is repelled by the damp parts. To the inked stone is pressed a paper to which is transferred by pressure the inked design.

In creating the original design, lithography obviously offers the artist a large amount of technical freedom. To be sure, he has to draw his image reversed – although this can be avoided by the use of lithographic transfer paper – but there is no resistance to his drawing instrument. The internal problem of lithography has been, therefore, much the same as that of serigraphy, the search for an identity – identity, or character, being established in art much as in life chiefly by limitations imposed, recognized, explored, contested, turned to account, and, occasionally, conquered. Theoretically there has been no solution to this problem, yet the problem itself may be more theoretical than real. We have already noted the remarkable qualities of Bavarian limestone in taking to itself both water and grease. The stone has the same taste for opposites in the matter of drawing upon it. The artist does have immense freedom and ease, yet the stone does leave its own mark upon the drawing. There is a grain to the stone and this affects the drawing both in lines and in broader areas, where a grainy gray modulates between black and white. At least to the spectator aware of the process, this grainy quality carries with it the weight of the stone itself and from this weight derives the identity of the lithograph as a medium. The highest degree of freedom for the artist's motion upon the stone combines with the drag of the stone itself to establish an individual proportion of unfettered flight to earthbound bulk.

This particular problem does not arise in connection with the older print methods. These are woodcut, engraving and etching, with their variants and auxiliaries. For classification these are divided into the relief process and the intaglio process. Lithographs, as long as we're being nomenclatural, constitute the

13.
Engraving. Copper plate, burins,
Prometheus by James Van Dyk,
state proof, 1960.

14.
WILLIAM HOGARTH, 1697-1764,
The Election (plate 1):
An Election Entertainment.
Engraving, 1755.

15.
Wood engraving.
Wood block, burins,
title page of *Passages from
the Book of Isaiah*,
illustrated by James Van Dyk,
1957.

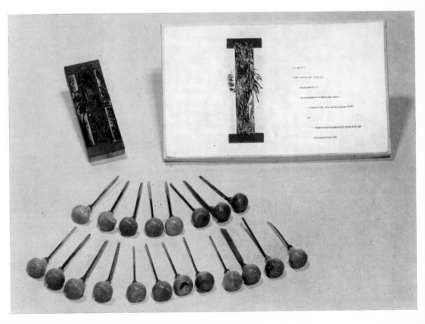

planographic process, and the lexicographic process has been used to maintain that serigraphs are planographic too, but this is doubtful.

Relief printing is so named because the area that prints stands up from the surface of which it is a part. Newspaper type is in relief from the slug in which it is cast. The great relief method and probably the oldest of all print methods is the woodcut. The woodcut is carved into a block of wood; and since it is a relief method, this means that the design to be printed isn't actually carved: it is carved around. To get one line in the print, the woodcutter's knife has to make two cuts, one along either side of the upstanding line. The image is therefore both reversed and negative. The cutting is done with extremely sharp knives and gouges and the block is turned fairly often during the cutting. Not only the sharp edges of the cutting tools but the grain of the wood is a factor in establishing the character of the medium. There is a tension between the grain and the cut, and this survives into the print even where the grain has been obliterated in the cutting. In some prints the grain is exaggerated before cutting by rubbing the block with a wire brush.

Printing the woodcut can be accomplished in any press or with no press by simply rubbing the paper against the inked block with a spoon. The image of the printmaker rubbing square inch after square inch with his spoon has the great advantage of conveying the importance of the printing process in prints. The whole business of applying the final pressure that transfers the drawing or design to the paper is very much a part of the act of creation. The woodcut artist printing one small area after another obviously has something close to total control of the printing process. This degree of control cannot be attained in a press.

Early woodcuts were colored by hand, some by stencil. True color woodcut, as in any of the other print processes, requires a separate block for each color, the blocks being keyed so as to register properly.

The chief variant of the woodcut is the wood engraving. The distinction is not as easy as you might think. Woodcuts are carved in the plank, usually working with the grain as much as possible. Wood engravings, by definition, are carved on the end-grain, that is, on a cross section of the wood. The quality of the grain in the cross section makes much finer work possible, and the degree of fineness – and a resulting hard precision – is the chief visual difference. Yet it is overwhelmingly clear that many of the early woodcuts obtained a very high degree of hardness and precision.

The intaglio processes are just the reverse of the relief processes. In relief, the line to be printed stands up on the block. In intaglio, the line to be printed is sunk into the plate. In a relief

16.

Etching. Zinc plate,
jeweler's rouge, nail,
screw, scissors, English burnisher,
Wounded Angel by
James Van Dyk, 1960.

17.

Etching.
Acid bath.

18.

Etching.
Printing press.

print, the printed line is an indentation in the paper. In an intaglio print, the printed line is raised from the paper. In most etchings and engravings this raised quality of the line can easily be seen by looking at the print from the side. The quality becomes even clearer if the print is lighted from the side rather than straight on. Often, the raised lines will actually cast shadows.

Engraving, the oldest of the intaglio processes, is accomplished by cutting into the polished surface of a metal plate, usually, copper. The cutting tool, or burin, is not as freely manipulated as the knives and gouges of the woodcutter. The burin is held steady, parallel to the body, and is pushed along the copper surface. Change of direction of a line is achieved not by turning the cutting edge, but by turning the plate. The engraver is thus constantly observing his work from changing points of view. As the burin is pushed through the copper, an edge is turned up out of the engraved line, just as a row of dirt is turned up by the plow making a furrow. This edge, called the burr, is removed with a scraper.

When the lines have been engraved and the burr removed, the plate is inked and again it is evident that the engraving enjoys a great increase of sophistication over the woodcut. The relief block is simply inked and printed. The engraved plate is subject to a great deal of variation and control. Ink is rolled onto the plate with a roller and then wiped off with a cloth and with the printer's hand. The ink thus remains in the engraved lines, not on the surface. The amount of ink in the lines can be controlled by *retroussage*, which is simply a partial wiping of the lines themselves. Also a very light film of ink can be left on the surface of the plate, producing, in the print, a smoky tone floating over the design.

Woodcuts can be printed by hand. Intaglio prints cannot. Inked plate, dampened paper, and a protective layer of felt blankets are passed together through a mechanical press. Under this pressure the ink is sucked out of the lines and the paper is pressed into the lines, resulting in the raised quality of lines in an engraving.

Pressure on a printing press is variable and less is used to print an etching than to print an engraving. Etching was developed early in the sixteenth century partly as a quick and easy substitute for engraving. The etcher does not have to cut into the copper plate as does the engraver. The lines are not cut, but eaten, or etched, by acid. The copper plate is first covered with an acid-resistant ground, which has been of various combinations of wax, asphaltum, varnish, and other substances. Etching ground needs two properties; it must adhere to the copper and it must resist the acid. Once the ground is applied, it is often smoked by flame for the convenience of the etcher; this gives him a dark

19.
LUDWIG MEIDNER, b. 1884,
Portrait of a Man.
Drypoint.

background against which his lines show clearly in a coppery sparkle.

The etcher draws on the ground with a needle, but any sharp point can be used. In the sixteenth century special tools were developed to imitate the quality of engraved lines, and in modern times etchers have used toothpicks and razor blades as their points. The effect of drawing upon the ground with a point is to lay bare the copper. When the drawing is complete the etched plate is immersed in a bath of acid and the acid – nitric, hydrochloric or others – eats into the exposed lines, not touching the parts protected by the ground. When the lines have been eaten deeply enough, the ground is removed from the plate and the etched plate prepared for printing much as is an engraved plate. As a cheap substitute for engraving, etching proved its value at once, but it soon revealed values of its own. The action of acid upon copper takes place in time; it is therefore subject to control by regulating the time. Furthermore, a stop-out varnish can be applied to some of the lines after a certain interval in the acid bath, to others after another interval and to others not at all, thus achieving a wide range of tones, from the most delicate wisp of a line to a deep, rich black where the lines merge in a darkly glowing shadow. When these values of etching were developed, the process passed far beyond its function of imitating engravings. Etching revealed a whole new range of subtlety and power to the printmaker. That range was further increased by new discoveries.

Only one of the new discoveries – mezzotint – ever became wholly dedicated to commercial practice and the reproduction of paintings or of scenes as such. Mezzotint is a very laborious process and that reason alone may account for its unpopularity among creative printmakers. In mezzotint, the copper plate is first uniformly roughened all over by the use of rockers that press points into the copper. If the plate were printed at that stage, the impression would show a smooth, velvety black. This roughened surface is then laboriously smoothed in the appropriate places by scrapers, burnishers, and abrasives. The areas completely smoothed, of course, print white and are the highlights of the picture. Almost without exception mezzotints exhibited in public or private print collections are eighteenth-century print copies of eighteenth-century paintings.

A much more fruitful addition to the vocabulary of the printmaker came from drypoint. As the name implies, the copper plate is drawn upon with a point – steel, diamond, or sapphire. The line thus scratched, however, is not the one that prints. The drypoint tool, like the engraver's burin, turns up a burr of raised metal alongside the scratched line and it is this burr, left on the plate, that takes the ink and prints the impression, an impression

20.
Aquatint-etching. Zinc plate,
resin bag, stop-out varnish,
brush, *The Bride* by
James Van Dyk, 1960.

21.
EUGÈNE DELACROIX, 1798-1863,
The Blacksmith.
Etching and aquatint, 1833.

of great richness, though one of great limitation because of the tendency of the burr to wear away rapidly under the pressure of the press. The burr can be strengthened by steel facing, applied electrolytically, a process also used to prolong the life of engraved and etched copper plates. Some lovely work has been done in pure drypoint, but generally it has been used in combination with etching and engraving.

This is true, too, of the other great augmentation of the intaglio process, aquatint. Aquatint is a form of etching in which the ground is used not to prevent the action of the acid on the plate, but to control it, thus producing, like mezzotint, an over-all tone, subject to variation. This is achieved by the use of a granular ground, usually of rosin. Powdered rosin, in the form of a dust, is fused to the heated plate. Since the ground is granular, when the plate is immersed in the acid, the acid eats at the plate between the grains of the rosin ground. As in line etching, aquatint is subject to the control of stopping out some portions and letting others endure a longer immersion in acid, thus making some areas dark, others light. Theoretically the degrees of light and dark are very many, but the great master of aquatint, Goya, usually employed only two or three. Even more than drypoint, aquatint is almost always used in combination with other processes, almost never used by itself.

Such are the principal tools and techniques of the printman. There are further variations, especially in etching. All of them, like the chief ones now reviewed, lean heavily toward indirection, toward sneaking up on an image, letting it emerge just when the artist seems preoccupied with something else. The complexities and the indirection inherent in the print processes all seem appropriate to the printmaker's basic and enduring attitude toward the world he finds himself in.

That attitude is clearly subversive, although many a first-rate printmaker has deceived himself and others into thinking that what he really wants to do is reform our vices. He doesn't at all. He wants to point them out, laugh at them, weep at them, shrug his shoulders at them, but above all to insist that they are there. This simple insistence goes with the professional detachment of the printman. The over-all attitude goes with the cutting of knives, the burning of acid, the quest for precision. The whole business sounds very negative compared to the joyous affirmations and sayings of Yes to life that ring through the history of oil painting, both in process and in presentation. Printmaking is negative, no doubt, but in the very fact that the plates, after all, are cut, and not only cut but printed, there is affirmation, the only one you get from most of the great printmen.

22.

ABRAHAM RATTNER, b. 1893,
Among Those Who Stood There.
Color etching and engraving, 1945.

In the Beginning: Love and Death

In the Beginning: Love and Death

Printmaking began in Germany and Italy sometime early in the fifteenth century. There was no Alois Senefelder for woodcut or metal engraving, or if there was he lacked the Bavarian's foresight in writing up a sympathetic account of his early struggles and monumental discoveries.

There was no need for a Senefelder. Not only the materials and tools for printmaking, but the processes themselves lay ready to hand and had been there for some centuries. As early as the sixth century the Copts of Egypt had actually used wood blocks to print designs on textiles, and textile printing from wood blocks was carried on throughout the Middle Ages in Europe. Engraving not only goes back to the Greeks, who cut designs into the backs of bronze mirrors, but back into prehistory, when engraving on bones was an art form along with cave painting. Ornamental and illustrative engraving on metal was practiced during the Middle Ages and was brought to a high state of facility and sophistication by early Renaissance goldsmiths. Etching, which did not become a print process until the last decades of the fifteenth century, was used by armorers much earlier.

All this had been in readiness for some time. Apparently the thing that tipped the scales and started printmaking was the arrival on the scene of cheap and plentiful paper. Parchment, which had served monks and monarchs in the Middle Ages, was not only expensive, but not very well suited to printer's ink. The Arabs had paper in the eighth century and the Moors brought it into Spain around the middle of the twelfth. Paper mills were established in Italy in the thirteenth century and in Germany in the late fourteenth. The missing ingredient had arrived and printmaking began. This rather simple-minded account raises more questions than it answers. For one, why didn't the Arabs invent printmaking? Why didn't the Europeans find out about paper earlier? And there is still a considerable gap between paper and prints. For those who like to play *Zeitgeist*, there is a world of material in the whole situation of the coming of prints.

For example, what is the relationship between prints and Protestants? Between prints and democracy? Between prints and principalities? The answer for all is the same: Ambiguous.

If there was ever a period that answered Dickens' well-known description of England in 1790, it was Germany and Italy as prints began to be made in the fifteenth century. The best of times and the worst of times could be found together anywhere you looked. In Italy this was the great age of painting. Beginning with Masaccio, a whole line of Florentine painters pushed forward the conquest of space, of movement, of weight and volume, of form and composition – a conquest reaching its culmination in the Vatican paintings of Michelangelo and Raphael. Also in Italy the fifteenth century was the great age of political corruption and

23.

ANONYMOUS ITALIAN,
*Head of a Man in a
Fantastic Helmet.*
Engraving, c. 1470-1480.

war as a private enterprise. The Church itself, guardian of Europe's spiritual values and guide to salvation for all mankind, was supported largely by a steady trade in spiritual goods, from appointments of archbishops to remission of punishment for sin. The Church was also engaged in another phase of its centuries-old struggle with the State; pope and emperor marched against each other and spun intricate webs of alliances.

Democracy? In both countries free cities had managed to maintain themselves for a couple of centuries. It was within the economic structure of those cities that the institution of printmaking speedily took its place, with production and sale strictly regulated by the guilds. Yet if printmaking was somehow related to those relatively democratic principalities, the relationship must have been that of the final flowering. For even as the printmen began their enterprise, the forces of the ancient feudalism and the new national tyranny were beginning their assault on city freedom. Old despotisms may have been dying in the birth days of prints, but new despotisms, even more despotic, were coming into existence.

Ever since the twelfth century the two great powers of Europe, Church and State, had been at war with each other; in the struggles between pope and emperor there had been room for free cities and free men to play one power against the other and thus preserve their own independence. Such maneuvering was a large part of the history of the free city of Florence, for example, and no less so of the free cities in Switzerland, along the Rhine and in the Lowlands. All the political, military and religious ferment of the fifteenth century, whatever its avowed aims, was moving toward the effective union of Church and State, to be accomplished in almost all countries of Europe by the middle of the sixteenth century. In states governed by such a union, there would be much less room for freedom of any kind. But before that union took place the fifteenth century established a tradition of free comment and criticism. Printmaking became part of that tradition from the beginning.

Partly this was due to the close association of printmaking with the literary wing of the "revival of learning" that had been in progress since the twelfth century. The new printing press brought forth new editions of Greek, Latin, and Scriptural classics. The new poetry and prose spread itself through science and philosophy, morality and storytelling, with the lines between the kinds by no means firmly established. The subversive note so evident in prints was also evident in the original works produced by the new scholars. Dante was an early, powerful example of the new learning's refusal to take the social order at its own evaluation and pictures for the *Comedy* were a continuing occupation of the printmakers. Boccaccio's works furnished another

24.
MICHAEL WOLGEMUT, 1434-1519,
Death Dance.
Woodcut.

25.
MASTER OF AMSTERDAM
(MASTER OF THE HAUSBUCH),
The Road to Calvary.
Drypoint, 15th century.

large source of printmaking and he too encouraged the realistic examination of authority by those subject to authority.

With the mention of Boccaccio another element comes into the background of early printmaking. This is death. The ten tales on each of ten days that make up the *Decameron* were told in 1348 by ten young refugees from the plague that gripped Florence. The plague had come in from the east and spread through Europe with horrible speed. There was no cure and no preventive measure that seemed to do any good. Thousands died in all countries and the experience remained a basic part of the intellectual background for generations. In printmaking specifically the plague was immortalized in the *Dance of Death*, the *Danse Macabre* or the *Totentanz* print series in which death was seen coming to all conditions and classes of mankind. The superb *Death Dance* by Dürer's teacher, Michael Wolgemut, chillingly expresses one prominent aspect of the theme, the lunatic delight of animated corpses and skeletons in rising from the grave, not in Christian glory but in grotesque glee in bringing death to others.

The theme is broadened by the Master of the Hausbuch in his drypoint of three kings meeting their dead predecessors who are also their future selves. The Hausbuch Master, one of the great semi-anonymous printmakers of fifteenth-century Germany, touches on the great theme of the time in *The Road to Calvary*, also in drypoint. The curving procession is seen most distantly simply as a jagged row of jagged points – standards and weapons – behind the rocky hill. The whole forward movement of the procession is carried by the rigid upright of the cross itself, under which Christ has fallen. The remarkable composition magnificently accomplishes one of the basic aims of German religious art at the time; the spectator is not allowed simply to observe; the whole subject and theme of the picture come spilling into his eyes. The course of the procession, the weight of the cross, the movements of the three brutal guards, all direct our eyes to the fallen Christ. He endures all, in contrast to the rage of the guards and the grief of Mary and John at the left. In further contrast to all of this, the line of the procession, that of the road in the foreground of the picture, sweeps without a halt, a low arc from left to right, its indifference culminated in the attendant with the coil of rope, his back turned to the whole incident on the way to death.

As with Italian painting, religion provided the vast majority of subjects for German printmaking. In fifteenth-century Germany there was great emphasis on the Passion of Christ, those events leading up to the death on the cross. Christ tried by Pilate, Christ beaten and mocked, Christ carrying the cross, Christ dying and dead, all received more attention than other subjects of scriptural derivation. The entire Old Testament was often represented only

26.
MASTER E. S., flourished 1450-67,
Man of Sorrows.
Engraving.

27.
ANONYMOUS (School of Ulm?),
Man of Sorrows.
Woodcut, colored by hand, c. 1460.

by Adam and Eve, whose sin created the need for the Crucifixion. From the first parents of mankind, print series would jump to the immediate ancestors of Mary, the mother of Jesus, pay relatively little attention to the career of Jesus as a teacher and devote the most time and thought to the last days.

The taste for violence found another outlet in the "Fourteen Auxiliary Saints," the canonized helpers of mankind in various special difficulties or special callings. The fourteen were all martyrs and their usual representations concentrated on the manner of their martyrdom. St. Sebastian was particularly popular because, having suffered death by arrows, he was the helper against the plague. The connections between the saints and their specialties was often rather strained. St. Sebastian, for example, was invoked against the plague by a kind of transfer of training. The old Roman god, Apollo, had been thought responsible for plague and Apollo carried a bow and arrows. St. Erasmus was a bishop of Antioch in Asia Minor, where he was killed in the fourth century. He became the patron saint of sailors apparently because he was executed by having his entrails pulled out of him and wound about a capstan, and a capstan, obviously, has to do with ships.

Before Dürer and his contemporaries, the chief German master was a printmaker known only as "E.S." from the initials he carved in many of his plates. His *Man of Sorrows with Four Angels* is a first-rate example of a kind of summing-up of the Passion of Christ in a single print of this title that was executed by many Germans of the period. The angels hold the instruments of torture and death used on Christ in the last few days. The theme reached one of its greatest expressions in the anonymous *Man of Sorrows* at the Chicago Art Institute. The angels are gone; the figure is cut off at the hips. The instruments of torture are still present but are completley subordinated to the details of suffering cut into the body. The emaciated torso plays compellingly against the compassion evident in the face, where sorrow more than suffering is in the lines.

Like most early printmakers. E.S. was a craftsman who did everything that came his way, including decorative lettering. The grotesque Q is in an ancient tradition of the illuminated manuscripts, except that it seems clearly to take note that the "lower orders" are lower chiefly because the higher orders ride over them. In startling contrast to the literary and artistic conventions of romantic love that have prevailed in other times and places, E.S. cut a *Garden of Love* that is realistic to the point of ribaldry. The figure eight that holds the composition like a frame sets off and contrasts the lascivious types in the foreground with the jousters in the background. The convention – still quite alive in the twentieth century – that the love of fair woman comes

28.

MASTER E. S.,
flourished 1450-67,
Fantastic Letter "Q".
Engraving, 1467.

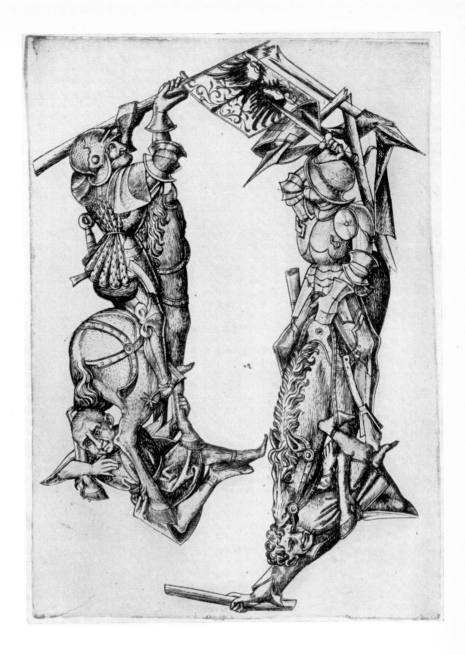

as a reward for deeds of derring-do is pulled apart by the eight-form of mountains, castle, and garden fence. In the upper oval the realists pursue a joust of their own with a way of their own. Their general spirit is perhaps symbolized in the hunting birds tied to the top of the fence and the falconer's gloves laid alongside. A bold bit of distortion ties the two scenes together. The top of the gate to the garden of love slopes up, part of the upper oval; the threshold slopes down with the lower. In any kind of perspective this is impossible, but the confidence with which it is perpetrated makes it work. The rich variety of engraved lines varies appropriately from the dull regularity of the trees around the tournament ground to the lush foliage under foot in the garden and the sensuous curves of the wood grain in the fence. Martin Schongauer, like E.S., was in the generation preceding Dürer. Schongauer died in 1491, probably about sixty years of age; Dürer was then nineteen and on his travels in Germany and Switzerland as a journeyman printmaker. Schongauer is the earliest German printmaker who is known to have been more active as a painter than as a goldsmith, a fact taken to fix his place as transitional; actually Schongauer is one of the earliest German printmakers to be known by name at all. His *Death of the Virgin* nevertheless has a quality that might be taken as left over from jeweler's engraving. Hands, drapes, forms, objects brought to the deathbed, the hair and arms of the Virgin herself, all are integrated in an endless and tireless flow of line. In later engraving a highly valued trick was the portrait or scene done without lifting the graver from the copper. Schongauer's death scene is not such a trick, but it does give something of the same feeling. The smooth energy behind the burin in its course through the turning plate is all preserved in the figures. All shades of emotional response are delineated and are paralleled by the complete range of deathbed consolations in the scene: candles, cross, prayerbooks, holy water, and the sprig of a plant.

Schongauer's twelve plates of the Passion became the models of many printmaker-copyists in Germany, Spain, the Netherlands and Italy. The *Agony in the Garden* erects a stone plinth as a center for the action. Beyond it come the soldiers and mob to take their Prisoner; Christ kneels at the plinth to behold the angel with the chalice of suffering; and before the plinth, posed right at the spectator, are the three sleeping apostles. The weight of their slumber is increased by the balancing mass of dark rock in the left background, related in shape both to the plinth and to the dead weight of the sleepers.

There was print activity in the Netherlands from an early date. Allaert du Hameel, architect and engraver, in a scene from the long march of the Israelites through the desert, had a subject beautifully suited to the turning qualities of the engraved line.

29.

MARTIN SCHONGAUER, C. 1430-91,
The Death of the Virgin.
Engraving.

30.

MARTIN SCHONGAUER,
The Agony in the Garden.
Engraving.

31.

ALLAERT DU HAMEEL, 1449?-1509?,
The Brazen Serpent.
Engraving.

The serpent was raised and the children of Israel paid it homage, doffing their hats like Netherlandish commoners to their betters. The coils of the adored image are repeated in the uncovered hair of the Israelites and come to lethal life in the real serpents attacking the men at the bottom of the picture. The rocky landscape is the barest of stages for the action of crime and punishment, with the latter emphasizing movement already latent in the former. In the upper corners the plate has decorations like architectural carvings and even these take on the serpentine coiling and flexing. The Gothic *'bosche* in the center indicates that Du Hameel probaly had the same home town – Hertogenbosch – as the painter, Hieronymus Bosch, who took its name as his own.

A complete architectural framework was used by Jacob Cornelisz van Amsterdam in his scenes from the *Life of the Virgin*. The arcs and circles frame the scenes as if on a carved wooden screen. The suggestion of ecclesiastical architecture is summed up in the central decoration dividing the two upper scenes of the Holy Family. Within this architectural carving, however, the scenes themselves open up to the suggestion of deeper space than the flat background of relief carvings. The principal scene, on the bottom, is interesting in its focus. On the left, the Virgin borne aloft by angels to where God awaits with a crown is a statement of an important Church doctrine, the Assumption. Cornelisz, in the spirit of his time, pushes this sacred event into the background to devote his main emphasis to the purely legendary incident of the burial of the Virgin. The funeral cortege is attacked by armed men brandishing points and blades, the weapons, essentially, of the woodcutter himself. One of the assailants has laid violent hands upon the coffin; the hands are violently – and miraculously – stricken from the aggressor and he falls to the ground, leaving his hands stuck to the cloth.

Printmaking in Italy never had anything like the importance it had in the north, for the excellent reason that heavy Italian patronage was being put into painting and the patronage was being richly rewarded. First-class talent went into painting. The artistic dynamo of Florence in the fifteenth century produced one great engraver, Pollaiuolo, and he produced, so far as we know for certain, one great engraving, the *Battle of the Nudes*. In the north of Italy there was Mantegna, but he was a painter first, a scholar and experimenter and avid collector of antiquities. Jacopo de' Barbari was a Venetian who was primarily an engraver, but to be so he emigrated to Germany, to Burgundy and the Netherlands; for a long time art history carried him on the books as a northerner, Jakob Walch.

Yet slight as top Italian production was, two of these three men created images that have endured as part of our common visual

32.

Three Naked Men Tied to a Tree.
Engraving.

33.

Sacrifice to Priapus.
Engraving.

34.

*The Apostles Carrying
the Coffin of the Virgin,*
from *The Life of the Virgin.*
Woodcut.

heritage, something that can be said of none of the Germans so far considered. And in the work of all three appears a sense of reality pretty much lacking in the more numerous northerners. Prints are always at least three things at the same time. They are arrangements of black marks on white paper; they are the record of certain movements of certain tools in certain materials; and they are images of a reality beyond ink and beyond the manipulation of instruments, which nevertheless comes into existence only in ink and by grace of such manipulation. In the early northern prints the first two things have been admirably present. The third has not been fully there. In the work of the Italians, the third thing, reality, springs to full life.

And it comes to life with no sacrifice of vigor. The vigor of line in the few Italian engravings is no less for being expressed with a strong grace that, so far, was simply unknown in the north.

Barbari's *Three Naked Men Tied to a Tree* convinces at a glance that the men are real, the trees are real, the ground, scarcely portrayed at all except as abstract lines, is solid earth. And the conviction takes place solely in line, with the lines of the large tree echoing the posture and the plight of the prisoners.

One cause of the Italian perfection is seen in Barbari's *Priapus* and in the *Bacchanal* and *Hercules* of Mantegna. This is the interest in classical myths and in the sculptural forms that embodied the myths. The north concentrated almost exclusively on the New Testament and, within that, on the Passion of Christ. In Italy to those persons and events were added the immense numbers of persons and events of both the Old Testament and the Old Romans. Also notable in Mantegna's plates is the background of diagonal lines. This suggests a constant flux in effective contrast to the monumentality of the figures. In Mantegna's masterwork of engraving, the *Madonna and Child*, this flux of lines continues, with a higher frequency, into the robes of the Madonna on the right, faintly suggesting that the tender image came from some process like the rubbing of ancient brasses.

Like Mantegna's *Madonna*, Pollaiuolo's single known engraving, the *Battle of the Nudes*, is one of the unforgettable images of European art. The figures themselves suggest some frightful finale to a gladiators' combat in ancient Rome. But the close-in background of foliage places the scene in a forest, cuts off any possibility of deep space, and forces all the details of the scene upon the viewer. Despite the objective horror of such a scene, it is not sheer carnage that impresses itself on the mind, but the tense energy of the bodies. Muscles, nerves, bones and bodies, all in swift and expert movement, are communicated in the nervous, sure line of the engraver. Not at all hidden in the carnage is the classical composition of the group, movement and impulse balanced against countermovement as in wrestling or in a sym-

35.
ANDREA MANTEGNA, 1431-1506,
Bacchanal with a Wine Press.
Engraving, c. 1490.

36.
School of Andrea Mantegna,
Hercules and Anteus.
Engraving.

phony. The blades of swords and axes, the points of daggers and arrows punctuate the strain of muscle. We feel the strain of arm and leg, of taut torso; we feel no less the pull of the bow, the weight of the ax. Through it all pulsates a human emotion — the joy of slaughter — we rarely acknowledge, at least nowadays. This part of the dark side of life is summed up in the superb understatement of the chain holding the two central warriors within striking distance of each other. Each holds the chain, obeying its deadly convention that they may not move to safety; but the convention of slaughter is unneeded; it hangs loose between the men.

37.
ANDREA MANTEGNA,
Madonna and Child.
Engraving, c. 1450–55.

38.
ANTONIO POLLAIUOLO, 1432?-1498,
Battle of the Nudes.
Engraving, after 1470.

Chapter Four

Albrecht Dürer
of Nürnberg

Albrecht Dürer of Nürnberg

Small, hard clouds scud across the sky, nearer to us than the larger clouds, just as hard, that roll like boulders. The sky itself is carved with black and white horizontal lines. From the upper left shoot crystalline rays from some light source out of sight above. In the top center an angel, lifted by powerful wings, passes over all, approving – it may be directing – the course and the carnage of the Four Riders below.

The Horsemen themselves are galloping in air, but the thin air offers all the resistance they need to chase down their course. The iron hoofs of their horses beat upon the air as if on stone. All of mankind fall beneath those hoofs, as inescapably as wheat beneath the scythe. Beneath those hoofs, in the lower right, the stages of fall are grouped: shocked surprise, protest, agony, despair, and death itself. Beneath those hoofs, in the lower left, the body of a bishop, face struck with horror, is swallowed by an obscene beast. The two barbaric kings, farthest away from us, ride upon mankind with the arrows of pestilence and the sword of war. In the foreground, Death on a pale horse is the image of famine, gaunt, emaciated, eyes burning in madness and the mission of slaughter. The great, robust central rider sets the pace for all four and swings the most deadly weapon of all, the lethal scales of final justice.

This powerful image of destruction is Albrecht Dürer's translation into cut lines of the vision described by Saint John in the Book of the Apocalypse, the mystical vision of the end of the world which is the final word of the New Testament. This image, published in 1498 and perhaps cut two years earlier, has been looked upon as heralding a new period of mortal strife in central Europe. The strife came, certainly, and lasted for almost a century and a half. The image, in the context of the *Apocalypse*, has been taken as heralding also the advent of the Reformation. It's an appealing thought, since it ties art and history together neatly; the notion is also attractive because it asserts the superiority of artists to theologians: if the Reformation began with the *Apocalypse* woodcuts, Dürer was twenty years ahead of Luther. The most important and the one uncontestable thing the *Apocalypse* illustrations herald is the arrival on the scene of the supreme master of the woodcut, Albrecht Dürer of Nürnberg.

Dürer was more than a master of the woodcut. He was a painter and an art theorist. He was a great engraver and a great draftsman. He may have invented etching and he was certainly one of the first artists to practice it. He was the closest thing to a Renaissance man that the north produced before Shakespeare. Over Shakespeare, Dürer had the advantage of actually living during the Renaissance. He knew the Italians, especially the Venetians, but also Raphael. He admired them and was admired by them. He exchanged prints with Raphael and Raphael is re-

39.
ALBRECHT DÜRER, 1471-1528,
The Apocalypse: The Four Riders of the Apocalypse.
Woodcut, 1498.

corded as believing that if only Dürer knew the antique, he would be the greatest of them all. By the standards of a Raphael, Michelangelo or a Leonardo, Dürer did not know classical art. By the prevailing standards of art in Germany, he was a classical artist-archeologist, though much of his classicism came to him secondhand, through his Italian friends. Insofar as genius can be accounted for by recipes, much of the unique vision of Albrecht Dürer comes from the all but unique combination of Italian grace and finesse with German intensity and introspection. On the whole, grace was in the service of intensity, rather than the other way round.

One of the great gifts Dürer brought back from an early visit to Venice was the sense of the single-sheet print. Printmaking in Germany started out as book illustration, as it did everywhere else. The Italians, as we have seen, were early able to make single prints that stood alone. This achievement, ordinary as it seems to us, loosened the association of prints with "printed matter". Dürer was able to make and sell prints that were purchased for themselves alone. Two early examples, executed probably just before the *Apocalypse*, are the *Martyrdom of the Ten Thousand Christians* and the *Martyrdom of St. Catherine of Alexandria*. The former organizes a scene of chaos and carnage so that the natural response to such a large-scale martyrdom is intensified by the apparent calm and cold-bloodedness with which the Christians are put to death. The great circle of torture and execution begins with the central group of bound victims being flogged with sharp points. Up to the left more Christians are being beaten up the slope toward another death, which we see in the top center, as soldiers with pikes and mace push the martyrs over the precipice. At the foot of the precipice, Christians are being decapitated. This circle of torment is stabilized by the group of dignified witnesses in the lower left and by the prone body of a bound bishop in the lower right, where a torturer is methodically boring through the prisoner's eye. The unnatural calm of the regally garbed group in the left, of the three witnesses at the bishop's death, and of the chatting pair on the right all add to the chill horror. Their calm, however, is but the figurative expression of the hard, quiet landscape itself and the hard, quiet, even lines of which it is made.

The strength of the lines is heightened in the *Catherine* scene, in part because of the more spectacular events taking place out of heaven and the frenzied reaction to those events by the spectators. As the saintly virgin goes to her death on the wheel that has since given her name to the standard firework, the skies open, as if ripped by a knife, and fire pelts down. Cloaks and hands are raised; horses falter and fall; men panic. Two figures retain their calm beneath the celestial fire: the martyr and her execu-

40.

ALBRECHT DÜRER,
*The Martyrdom
of the Ten Thousand Christians.*
Woodcut, 1494.

41.

ALBRECHT DÜRER,
The Martyrdom of St. Catherine.
Woodcut, 1498.

42.

ALBRECHT DÜRER,
*The Apocalypse:
The Martyrdom of St. John.*
Woodcut, 1498.

tioner. The distant landscape is also calm, its clear lines in sharp contrast to the scored surface of the hill directly behind the saint. Everywhere the quality of the cut line coincides with the quality of the moment portrayed. Fire drops from heaven like melting rocks; the feel of the flames that leap from the wheel of death is indistinguishable from the blades imbedded in the wheel. Despite his grim calm, the executioner himself, as his fifteenth-century stripes are translated into cut lines, seems almost a diagram of nerves stretched taut to the point of lethal action.

The *Apocalypse*, of course, was not independent of a story. The story for which Dürer's fifteen woodcuts are illustration is the end of the world, a theme that, in one way or another, has never been completely absent from printmaking through the centuries. Dürer opens the story with two views of the author, St. John. The first is taken not from the Book of the Apocalypse, but from Christian tradition, according to which the author of the fourth Gospel suffered martyrdom but did not die under it. He is subjected to boiling oil and, despite the efforts of executioners with ladle and bellows, he prays and remains alive. Dürer employs a remarkable pictorial device to crowd our attention in upon the saint. The distant view is blocked out completely by the looming castle. The top line of the castle is the same, visually, as the farther line of the draped canopy. Thus the bulking strength of the mighty fortress is pulled into the foreground by the forced perspective of the cloth. Behind the ruler seated at the left, the elaborate tapestry performs a somewhat similar function; its plane is projected through the ruler and his retinue: everything leads to the saint. The lines of the saint's face are the strongest in the scene, an effect against normal perspective but very much in order with the desired emotional response to the scene.

Having shown St. John as he appeared to the mighty of earth, the artist contrasts the prophet's plight with his heavenly vision, the beginning of the vision which is the Book of the Apocalypse. In the *Martyrdom* every inch of the picture surface is occupied by line; in the *Vision*, the open spaces of heaven are part of the vital rhythm between the seer and what he sees. God sits on a rainbow turned to crystal, hard and fixed in the heavens. Seven is a mystical number and, with twelve, figures in many details of the Book. St. John kneels before God in the circle of seven candlesticks, all the same, yet each different. The hand of God holds seven stars, and the stars, in the hard medium of the woodcut, seem cut from burning rock rather than formed of pure light. From the mouth of God issues forth not the breath of the spirit but the sword of divine justice and retribution, which is a major theme of the Book.

After the Four Riders, the sword of God next appears multiplied

43.

ALBRECHT DÜRER,
*The Apocalypse: St. John's
Vision of Christ
and the Seven Candlesticks.*
Woodcut, 1498.

44.

ALBRECHT DÜRER,
*The Apocalypse:
Four Angels Staying
the Winds and Marking
the Chosen.*
Woodcut, 1498.

45.

ALBRECHT DÜRER,
*The Apocalypse:
The Seven Trumpets
Are Given to the Angels.*
Woodcut, 1498.

and ready in the hands of four angels. A fifth marks the foreheads of the faithful, as the doorposts of the Israelites were marked in Egypt against the passage of Death, as the foreheads of Christians are marked on Ash Wednesday that they may remember Death. Here begins a fast, movie-like sequence, one of the great advantages of printmaking over painting. The four sword-bearing angels are repeated in the clouds with the four winds of heaven, indicating the scope of the angelic slaughter. Then, in the next print, God distributes the horns of the Last Judgment to angels. The horns are blown, fire falls again from heaven, the sun and the moon are disturbed and the whole surface of the earth writhes in waves, cataclysms, explosions and falling stars.

In the following scene, with a change analogous to the camera's dollying back and changing our view of the same scene, heaven has retreated somewhat; our focus is upon earth, with the four destroying angels laying about them with the swords of God. Popes and princes fall beneath their blows. There are riders in the sky and the trumpets never cease their noise. The extraordinary balance of the composition is built on a vertical axis from Dürer's monogram to God in heaven. The heavenly altar and the earthly distant castle are points on this pole; from it the figures festoon out and in: angels, riders, swords, and the earth littered with the slaughter of the guilty.

After another image of St. John during his vision – thus maintaining the frame of the story – Dürer introduces the second major pictorial theme, the beast with seven heads, a symbol with as many interpretations as there are interpreters. Its tail reaches to the stars, which, again, resemble burning snow crystals. The chief head of the beast vomits upon the earth. The beast is opposed by the "woman clothed in the sun," traditionally interpreted as the Virgin Mary. Blessed by God, she stands upon the crescent moon, is winged and has a crown of twelve stars.

Next St. Michael and his angelic army battle with the beast, which is cast out of heaven. Again the simple outlines of village, forest, sea and mountains are contrasted with the heavily lined image of the battle in the sky.

The beast now appears upon the earth and the lines establish an equal balance between heaven and earth. Above, God holds the sickle of harvest. So does the upper angel on the right. The lower angel, carrying the cross, brandishes a sword. From the clouds of heaven comes a rain of blood from which emerges a companion monster to the great beast with seven heads. The beast itself is so firmly established on earth that it has its worshipers, among them princes and popes.

Again there is an interlude of St. John and his vision, this time of the blessed, with palms, worshiping the Lamb of God. Then Dürer cuts back to the beast in its most dreadful apparition, with

46.
ALBRECHT DÜRER,
The Apocalypse:
Battle of the Angels.
Woodcut, 1498.

47.

ALBRECHT DÜRER,

The Apocalypse:
St. John Devours the Book.
Woodcut, 1498.

48.

ALBRECHT DÜRER,

The Apocalypse: The Sea Monster
and the Beast
with the Lamb Horns.
Woodcut, 1498.

49.

ALBRECHT DÜRER,

The Apocalypse:
St. Michael Fighting the Dragon.
Woodcut, 1498.

50.

ALBRECHT DÜRER,

The Apocalypse: The Adoration
of the Lamb and the Hymn
of the Chosen.
Woodcut, 1498.

51.

ALBRECHT DÜRER,

The Apocalypse:
The Woman of Babylon.
Woodcut, 1498.

the scarlet woman, the Whore of Babylon, seated on its back. Earth and heaven alike are filled with dynamic lines and fearful events. The beast itself is backed up by flame. The Whore raises a chalice "of mystery" to the deluded mankind which worships her. A distant city is destroyed by fire from heaven as overhead two great angels grieve that mankind forgets its salvation to worship the Whore. Meanwhile to the left of the angels the whole heavenly horde, led by the Four Riders, prepares for the final battle, the final cleansing of the earth by fire and sword. Throughout the picture the motive of twisting forms acts as a constant frame and accompaniment for all the events. The leaves of the foreground foliage have that twist, as do the tongues of devouring fire in the background and the piles of clouds that mount from heaven to earth enclosing the riders of the sky.

Dürer closes the series as St. John closes his book, with the prophetic saint given a vision of the New Jerusalem come down from Heaven. In the upper right an angel points out the city to St. John. The city itself is a vision of calm and order, with angels at the gates and flights of birds overhead. Significantly, however, both the New Jerusalem and St. John in the vision are in the background. The foreground is occupied by the last act of divine retribution against Satan. The beast is thrust under the earth into flames by an avenging angel holding the key to Hell.

The Passion of Christ became for Dürer as it had been for his predecessors a main preoccupation. He completed five sets and was working on a sixth when he died. Begun about the time of the *Apocalypse* but not completed and published until 1511, his *Great Passion* in woodcut affords material for comparisons in the evolution of an artist's style. In the *Agony in the Garden*, one of the first seven plates, the whole scene is bristling with points and blades formed by the edges of rocks, sprouting trees and the weave of the fence in the distance. In *Christ Bearing the Cross*, Dürer produces the effect of the whole population of Jerusalem pushing Jesus through the gates of the city toward death. As in several of the *Apocalypse* plates, the center of the scene glistens with dramatic contrasts of white and black. The first impression of the area behind the fallen Jesus is one of great confusion, but there is implacable order in it all. Veronica, Simon, St. John, and the Virgin Mary are easily identifiable as are various functionaries of the excution. The chaos comes from the strokes of the knives in the wood and not from the figures themselves. In the five cuts done some twelve years later to complete the series, Dürer's line has been refined enormously. This is immediately evident in *The Last Supper*, where the intersecting arches of the ceiling are in some measure an abstraction of the human composition below. *Christ in Limbo* depicts the visit of Christ to

52.

ALBRECHT DÜRER,
*The Apocalypse:
The New Jerusalem.*
Woodcut, 1498.

Hell between the Crucifixion and the Resurrection. The souls of the just, imprisoned until Christ's atonement by death, are released and surge hopefully up out of their dungeons. The demons, hideous to look upon, are powerless. Adam and Eve stand holding the cross; Christ's own banner of Resurrection is in the same oblique plane as the cross and creates, in the wind of morning, an arch of its own to place against the stone arch of Hellgate. While the halo of Christ in the earlier plates was made of black lines, here it is made of white light, a reversal of the normal woodcut process and a minor indication of Dürer's complete mastery.

Drawing itself was a passion with Dürer; so was the measurement of man. For years he was convinced there was a hidden secret to drawing as there was to nature, and he recorded his extreme gratitude to Jacopo de' Barbari for a set of proportions for the human body. While the great Italian artists were studying the structure and movements of the human body, Dürer concentrated on its proportions. He haunted the public baths of Nürnberg and made drawings of the human figure there revealed.

The woodcut of the *Men's Bath* also contains, in the figures of the four bathers, representations of the "four humors" of late medieval psychology: from left to right, ignoring the watcher and the two musicians, these are melancholic, choleric, sanguine, and phlegmatic. The melancholic, leaning on the post, is thought to be Dürer. It is significant that, even immersed in his draughtsman's studies of the human body, Dürer was concerned with something beyond the look of things. The "humors" may be a clumsy theory of psychology, but they helped make up to the Nürnberg artist for what the Italians were deriving from anatomy. The engraving of *Four Witches* is somewhat equivalent to the male humors in their bath. Again Dürer aims at more than mere nude studies. In so aiming, according to some authorities, he gets considerably less. It is true that there is rarely a shred of voluptuous appeal in Dürer's nudes. His avowed goal is the depiction of life as it is, seen coolly without the distorting glass of desire. The quest for precision was its own passion, as may be seen in Dürer's various pictures of drawing machines. His celebrated woodcuts of a master and his helper drawing a lute and of an artist drawing a greatly foreshortened nude woman, in each case with the aid of a machine for drawing, show a passion for design that has nothing to do either with sex or music.

One happy fruition of Dürer's love for proportion is his great print of *Adam and Eve*. We see immediately the increased flexibility of line and variety of tone that Dürer derived from engraving as compared to woodcuts. Behind the two figures a subtle range of dark tones shows the depths of the forest. In the depths we pick out the figures of the friendly animals of Paradise before

53.
ALBRECHT DÜRER,
The Great Passion:
Christ Bearing the Cross.
Woodcut, pub. 1511.

54.

ALBRECHT DÜRER,
The Great Passion:
The Agony in the Garden.
Woodcut, pub. 1511.

55.

ALBRECHT DÜRER,
The Great Passion:
The Last Supper.
Woodcut, 1510.

56.

ALBRECHT DÜRER,
The Great Passion:
Christ in Limbo.
Woodcut, 1511.

the time of the Fall of Man. Leaves, bark, fruit, animal fur and human skin all take on a distinguishing texture. The conventional covering of the sex organs is unnecessary, really, for in this perfectly proportioned pair there is a human beauty that goes beyond sex. The ominous moment we recognize from the Book of Genesis, but Dürer has added, in the far upper right, a mountain goat poised precariously on cliff-edge. There is a goat, too, behind our first parents, but the strongest premonition of ill is also the subtlest, the dark of the forest behind the couple.

The female nude is seen without glamor and yet with an almost hypnotic fascination in Dürer's engraving of *The Great Fortune*. Balancing on a globe, the bulky woman walks the air above a city lost in the mountains. The tiny inhabitants go about their ways unsuspecting of the passage in the air of the mysterious figure. Like the Whore of Babylon, she holds aloft a chalice, but the total significance is less clear. Winged, she carries harness and bridle – for what mount? The coil of cloud lifts like a veil to reveal the town below and Fortune above. The print itself reveals explicitly something implicit in Dürer's religious prints, that he is capable of going beyond the received interpretations of Christianity for the expression of his own view of life. Nothing is more alien to all varieties of Christianity than the ancient idea of Fortune, whether she is considered the pagan goddess or the ultimate agnosticism. Dürer, throughout his life and throughout his work, was genuinely devoted to the Christian revelation. A fervent admirer of Luther, he had great hopes of reform and saw them dashed on the political, or perhaps simply human, realities that soon took charge of the Reformation. His final ecclesiastical conclusion was that "the new Evangelical knaves made the Popish knaves seem pious by contrast." As in the *Apocalypse* and the intensely personal prints of the *Passion of Christ*, Dürer in *The Great Fortune* powerfully expressed the nature, often felt to be true, of the way life is.

His two supreme engravings explore still further the world of religious feelings somewhat outside the realm of orthodoxy. *Knight, Death and the Devil* was done early in Dürer's service to the Emperor Maximilian, the "last knight of Europe," but the great engraving was not done for the emperor. For Maximilian Dürer worked on vast and vain print projects designed to transform woodcut, like painting, from a popular art to the obedient servant of political power. Like numerous artists of his time, Dürer tried his hand at designs for fortifications. *Knight, Death and the Devil* may or may not have been suggested by the emperor; certainly there is no explicit reference. The theme itself goes well back into medieval morality literature and art, but in Dürer's engraving there is a sense of obsolescence about the knight accompanied by Death and the Devil. Dürer, disciple of what the eye sees, has even captured what the ear hears: we expect the armor

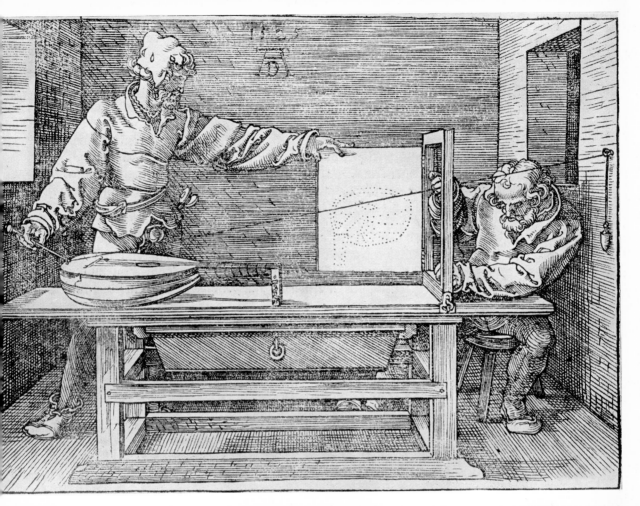

59.
ALBRECHT DÜRER,
Master and Helper Drawing a Lute.
Woodcut, 1525.

60.
ALBRECHT DÜRER,
Artist Drawing a Nude Woman.
Woodcut, 1538.

62.
ALBRECHT DÜRER,
The Great Fortune.
Engraving, c. 1501-1502.

63.
ALBRECHT DÜRER,
Melancholy.
Engraving, 1514.

61.
ALBRECHT DÜRER,
Adam and Eve.
Engraving, 1504.

to creak. The horse is wonderfully sturdy, but the knight rides into a dusk more gloomy and more certain than the end of day. The armor may be proof against the schemes of the malformed Demon and even against the direct attack of Death, but the skull is on the stump before the horse; the silent fall of sand is held before the knight's eyes. Doom is in his face, in his carriage, and in the fine web of lines the artist has thrown over almost every spot beneath the sky.

The sky itself is caught in the web of "Melencolia." It is important to bear in mind that the name does not mean simply a downcast mood, but rather a human type, the type Dürer thought himself and the type, according to the theory of humors, to which artists belonged by nature. Dürer was inquisitive, a student of everything that came his way and quite willing to go out of his way to see something curious, instructive, or unusual. He sits here, in spirit, heavy yet not a lump, surrounded by the instruments and symbols of the studies he pursued. Making and measuring may be taken as the two chief branches of his profession as interpreted by the artist himself, and the scene of *Melancholy* is cluttered with everything needed for making and measuring. A carpenter's tools are near the bottom edge. Up the left edge are an inkwell, a hammer, and a crucible set in fire. Half-hidden by Melancholy's skirts are a bellows and a pincers. She holds a calipers, resting her hand on a book, and carries a full complement of keys. The calipers measure space, the hanging scales measure weight, the glass of sand measures time. Beyond the strange, ornamental bat with the title, a falling comet covers the sky with its rays.

The most abstract instrument of measure and study in the picture is the polygonal figure, but something of its disposition of bulk and plane is made specific in the brooding figure of Melancholy herself. For she sits, surrounded by the tools of her trade and with natural and abstract objects for contemplation. Lost in thought, she is by no means overly optimistic about the end results of either thought or life. This is a conclusion more or less natural to a printmaker whose achievement is in the making of a print and in what measure it takes of life.

64.
ALBRECHT DÜRER,
The Knight, Death and the Devil.
Engraving, 1513.

Chapter Five

After Dürer

After Dürer

It's odd that Dürer never took up one of the great print themes of his time, the *Dance of Death*. In the traditional subjects the Nürnberg master handled, such as the *Passion*, the *Life of the Virgin* and the *Apocalypse*, he impressed upon them something of his own intensity and brought to complete realization the feelings about these themes inherent in the work of earlier German printmakers. A comparable realization for the *Dance of Death* was achieved by Dürer's younger contemporary, Hans Holbein of Augsburg, Basel, and London.

There were twenty-six years between Dürer and Holbein. Holbein's career forcefully illustrates what a profound difference those years made for the Central European artist. Dürer arrived at artistic maturity in the nineties of the old century; Holbein, in the 1520s. What happened in the meantime and continued to happen as Holbein grew in mastery, was the success of the Reformation. The new religion had epochal effects on art, devastating or liberating, depending on your point of view, and actually both at once. The Swiss Puritanism at Basel rather frowned on art in general and particularly on religious art, which is what most artists of the time had been trained to do. From this buyer's market that wasn't buying, Holbein emigrated to England where he made a brilliant if brief career painting the newly rich and newly powerful of Henry VIII's court. The German artist became the first in an illustrious line of British portrait painters.

Thus, even more dramatically than Dürer's, Holbein's career marks the change in European life and art from the Madonna to the millionaire. Between the two, while still at Basel, Holbein created the *Dance of Death*.

The series of forty-one cuts, each roughly two by two and a half inches, is quite different in feeling from both Holbein's early religious sentiments and his later, cold-eyed pomp and circumstance in England. The subject, of course, goes well back into the Middle Ages, but Holbein's angle of view, mental as well as visual, is all his own and all new. Traditionally, the *Dance of Death* is a grim subject, intended to induce salutary feelings of apprehension about the approaching end for us all. Holbein invests the whole performance with irony and playful humor. We no longer shudder; we smile, and we smile without for a moment doubting the basic premise that Death does indeed come to all men. Holbein's earlier German and Swiss customers took God and the saints and angels with total seriousness; his later English customers took themselves with profound seriousness. In the *Dance of Death* Holbein doesn't really take anything with complete seriousness. Death is a comedian and an extremely skillful one.

This attitude is Western man's most precious heritage from Renaissance humanism, more important than the revival of classical Latin or the beginnings of modern science. All through the bloody

65-72.
HANS HOLBEIN, 1497-1543,
Alphabet of Death.
Woodcuts, c. 1524.

and serious events of the humanist centuries, this stream of silvery laughter runs from Boccaccio to Erasmus and Thomas More to Rabelais and Cervantes. The attitude of humanist laughter received its most notable graphic expression in the *Dance of Death*. Holbein was a friend of Erasmus, having illustrated his *Praise of Folly*. When, a migratory worker in the arts, Holbein left the depressed area of Basel, he carried a letter of recommendation from Erasmus to Thomas More, humanist wit and chancellor of England.

Holbein had a kind of rehearsal for the *Dance of Death* in designing an *Alphabet of Death* to be used as a printer's initial letters. There are twenty-four letters; "I" doubles as "J" and "V" as "U." The blocks are one inch square. The scope of Death's stage is physically limited, but Holbein achieved humor and characterization in these postage-stamp-sized drawings. They amply repay study with a magnifying glass, less for the astonishing authority of the minuscule lines than for the full flavor of the tableaux.

The letters themselves – plain, Roman forms – constitute an additional hazard for design. The encounters have to be fitted not only into a square inch but into a square inch already occupied. Holbein met that challenge magnificently. The disposition of Death, his fellows, and his victims seems perfectly natural; there are none of the grotesque distortions common in earlier illuminated manuscripts, but the figures never get in the way of the letters. The letters, on the other hand, introduce a value of their own. Anyone who knows the alphabet automatically reads them in sequence and moves swiftly from one to the next. An arbitrary but effective movement is thus imposed on the series.

The Alphabet opens with the grisly musicians, presented like an orchestra tuning up before the performance. The skeletons immediately sound the theme of no respect for person or office. Two of them, assisted by a small demon, drag off the pope, tipping his tiara and tugging his cape. The emperor is attacked, fights back and loses his crown. A king falls on all fours and is ridden like a horse. A cardinal is plucked. Death lewdly lifts the skirt of the empress and rudely takes the necklace off the queen. Like pope and cardinal, the bishop is dragged away by his ecclesiastical robes. There is a saucy impudence about Death throughout. In I, he's in costume; in K, he trips up his victim; he mocks the priest in L, and the scholar in M. The money changer is hard at work in N, when his gold is rattled by the hand of Death. In P, Death engages in battle with the soldier, and, in Q, robes himself decorously to lead away the nun. The jester of R is not at all sympathetic to the final jest, but in S, Death becomes a lover, slips a hand of bones into a fair bosom and a finger along a white thigh. And so goes the dance: the drunkard, down and out, has one final drink poured into him; the rider discovers an unexpected companion, the card-

Der Cardinal.

Der Artzet.

Die Edelfraw.

Der Edelmann.

player, an unexpected winner taking all. There are variations of mood in the last letters. In W, Death seems a happy arrival to the aged monk; in Y, Death's easy assumption of the role of playful parent has a touch of horror.

The series concludes with a Last Judgment, notable chiefly for accommodating the entire population of the world on a postage stamp. The whole series gives the effect of the *Dies Irae* on the head of a pin — to music with a ragtime beat.

Having warmed up with the ABCs, Holbein cleared his stage of the letters, expanded it to something like five times the space of the initials, and opened up the flatline background to disclose appropriate settings for those chosen by Death. *Dance of Death*, by the way, while it is the title by which the series has been known for something over four hundred years, is not the original. That was *Images and Storied Aspects of Death* when the forty-one cuts were published in 1538 and it has rarely been heard since then. In the *Dance* itself the irony of the *Alphabet* is intensified and even conventionalized; Death arrives at each scene just as the victim is at the peak moment in some typifying action; Death arrives as often as not in garb or gesture that belongs to the scene, thus making it a burlesque. Throughout the series Death's hourglass, signal that the time has come, turns up in ever changing positions and so lends another combination of unity and variety to keep things moving and keep them together in the mind.

The series opens with a few swift scenes from Paradise, establishing the fact that Death came into the world when Adam sinned. Playing the viol, Death leads the couple out of the Garden and lends a hand to Adam's efforts at clearing the ground. Then the skeletons gather, as in the *Alphabet*, tune up their instruments, and the *Dance* begins.

It begins, as in the smaller series, with doom at the top. Death takes the pope just as he places a crown on a king, who kneels to kiss the papal foot. Among the assembled churchmen is a second skeleton, robed as a cardinal. It is then the turn of the emperor, who is taken as he is himself administering justice. The king sits at table and Death pours himself a drink. The cardinal enthroned hears a petition, but between the hearing and the decision, Death snatches off the broad-brimmed hat of churchly power. The queen walks in procession and Death takes her by the arm and points out the grave that yawns at her feet. The *Dance* continues down through the orders of society, spiritual and temporal. As it does, three major themes emerge. The first of course, is the one laid in so strongly in the opening cuts of death in high places, Death comes to all men. This was the traditional point of all the old death pictures; it was used to get people to come to church and is used today to get people to buy

79.
HANS BALDUNG (GRIEN), 1476-1545,
The Witches.
Woodcut, 1511.

80.
HANS BALDUNG (GRIEN),
The Bewitched Groom.
Woodcut, 1522.

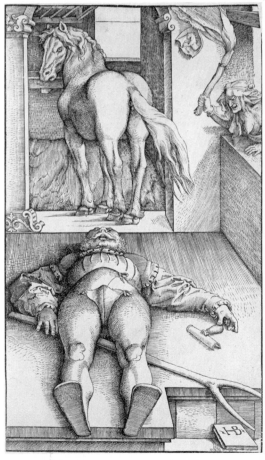

insurance. The theme, however commercialized, is essential to anyone's understanding of his own life.

The second theme is the satiric one of Death as retribution on the powerful who use their power injustly. The Advocate and the Counsellor are both shown doing profitable business with the rich while the poor ask in vain for justice. This theme is extended in the Nun's cut, an instance of exquisite timing. On her knees, she turns from her lute-playing lover to her religious duties and, just as she does, Death snuffs out the candle.

Death as the wished-for release from care is the third theme. It is presented most eloquently in the figure of the Old Man, whom Death courteously helps into the grave, and in the figure of the Plowman, whom Death aids by whipping the wornout nags on toward the distant end of the final furrow.

More mode than theme is the relish, humor, and cheerful enthusiasm with which Death does his duty. Almost all the victims are standing, sitting, or moving very slowly. Death is in violent motion everywhere. And he enjoys himself. "Up, up, sweet slug-abed," he seems to cry to the Duchess, as his companion fiddles away. He joins the Countess in her dressing room and gaily contributes a necklace of old bones to her adornment. As in the *Alphabet*, Death's final call is for a little child, whom he takes off by the hand as if for a day's outing, while the impoverished mother and sister shriek their unheard protest.

The backgrounds shift from scene to scene, indoors, outdoors, a palace, a hovel, the town, the country. They give form to the space in which Death acts; they underline the primary motif; and, in their incessant changing, they at once reveal and enhance the artist's great contribution to the art of the print. For what Holbein has actually done in the *Dance of Death* is to invent the motion picture as a visual narrative. The singleminded energy with which Death leaps through the scenes is the energy of the movie. Indeed the essence and the rhythm of the whole series were embodied whole in many of the early silent comedies of French and American movie makers. The incidents of the "chase" sequence, in which the fleeing hero hurtles through milieu after milieu, completely upsetting the order that obtained before his arrival, are like those of the *Dance* in the appropriateness of the intruder to the scene he intrudes upon and in the total catastrophe he brings. The difference is that, for Holbein, neither appropriateness nor catastrophe was accidental.

Another contemporary of Dürer's, and one much closer to him than Holbein, was Hans Baldung (Grien). Baldung studied with Dürer, and of all the artists who worked with the Nürnberg printmaker, Baldung is by far the most original. Technically, he was one of the first artists to experiment with color prints. More interesting are the ends to which he put his increased command.

81.

HANS BALDUNG (GRIEN),
Adam and Eve.
Chiaroscuro woodcut, 1511.

82.

HANS BALDUNG (GRIEN),
Aristotle and Phyllis.
Woodcut.

The Witches is a chiaroscuro woodcut, made by overprinting a tone block on top of the block carved with the design. By boldly reversing the normal expectation of black on white, Baldung has evoked the very spirit of his subject, a subject, incidentally, which indicates a tendency of his time to be tired of reason and turn to direct supernatural manipulation. The pursuit of witches became a European pastime, eventually spreading to Massachusetts. Baldung's *Bewitched Groom* is a memorable image of the belief in witches and their dire effects. The drastically foreshortened groom sweeps up into the picture to be stopped by the horse's bulk. The scrawny witch observes and somehow Baldung conveys the impression that the foreshortening itself is part of the cast spell. Baldung's woodcut of *Adam and Eve* is notable for its implication that the original sin of humanity was sex rather than disobedience. Along with witchcraft, and by no means unrelated to it, this notion was taken up by the new age just dawning, and it, too, found its way to New England. Witchery and bitchery combine with the rejection of classical reason in Baldung's *Aristotle and Phyllis*. The ancient philosopher most revered by the Middle Ages in seen crawling on his hands and knees down the garden path. Seated side-saddle on his back is his wife, no Venus certainly, but none is needed: the simple fact of female flesh is enough to reduce the noblest of minds to miserable animality. Pleased with herself, Phyllis flogs her man daintily and keeps a tight hold on the reins. High above, leaning over the wall, is a calm observer – the artist, perhaps – who is not in the least surprised.

Meanwhile, in the Netherlands, printmaking was developing some other variations on the general printman's theme of the underside of things. One such variation is seen in some of the engravings of an extraordinarily gifted artist, Lucas van Leyden. Child prodigy, friend and assiduous student of Dürer, Lucas became one of the most influential printmakers who ever lived, but this was more on technical than artistic grounds. Along with his contemporary, the equally influential Marcantonio Raimondi, Lucas devised the beginnings of a standard look and a standard process for engraving. This has been variously regarded as a high achievement and a tragedy. Standardization of line made for ease in reproducing paintings and actual scenes, and to these lowly functions printmaking espoused itself as soon as it became clear there was money to be made.

At any rate, in Lucas' own work, his standardized look isn't all that standardized and often the extreme delicacy of his lines lends a touch of understatement to the general mood of the engraving. This is so in *Calvary, Ecce Homo* and that curious print, *The Dance of the Magdalene*. In *Calvary*, the central event is relegated to the deep background and our attention is called to the goings

83.

LUCAS VAN LEYDEN, 1494-1533,
Calvary.
Engraving, 1517.

84.

LUCAS VAN LEYDEN,
Ecce Homo.
Engraving, 1510.

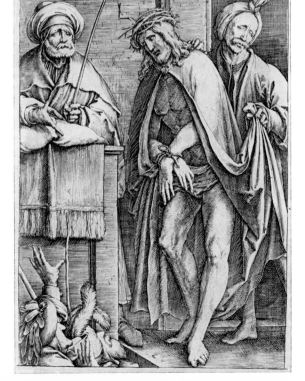

on in the foreground, the most notable of which is in the lower left, where the soldiers battle over the seamless garment. Other groups chat or simply pass by while the chief mystery of Christianity is being enacted above.

This focus on indifference, very quietly stated, is still quiet but nevertheless stronger in *Ecce Homo*. The scene is the one in the Gospels, painted or carved a thousand times, in which Pilate, still trying to please everyone, presents his Prisoner to the crowd. Usually representations of the scene concentrate on two aspects: the horrible wounds of Christ and the equally horrible cry of the crowd for blood. Lucas does neither. We see the crowd more clearly than we see Christ, and, to be sure, hands are raised in the traditional demand for blood. But the real point of the engraving is made by the sheer distance that separates the crowd from Christ. Perspective is exaggerated and there seems to be no real relationship at all between the crowd and Christ. The complete calm and indifference of the people most to the foreground underlines the effect, which is subtly strengthened by the cool studies in perspective across the entire background.

In *The Dance of the Magdalene*, this comment on human indifference is quite explicit, but the comment is made without any moral signpost. The situation is presented and the viewer asked to draw his own conclusion even if it be but a shrug for the way of the world. The great reformed sinner of the New Testament returns to, presumably, the haunts of her days of high living. Nothing has changed. A hunt, conceivably symbolic, goes on in the background, and, in the foreground, to the music of fife and drum, couples are sporting in the shade. Is the comment on the world, that it's always up to its old tricks, or on saints, that they think gay dogs can learn new ones?

By the middle of the sixteenth century the reduction of engraving to a system received a great boost from the establishment of print publishing houses run by entrepreneurs rather than either printers or artists. One of the most successful was Hieronymus Cock, of Antwerp, who employed a group of engravers, a group of designers, and even a group of artists unconcerned with design, to turn out his goods for an increasing public. Landscapes were popular; so were little "moralities," illustrations of folk sayings or the precepts of religion. The star of Cock's show was a fellow Fleming who later became famous as a painter, Pieter Bruegel, the elder. The evolving process in an establishment like Cock's was for the artist to work in response to what today would be called a market survey. The designer then translated the artist's picture into a design for an engraving; the engraver cut this into metal. At times the process was further elaborated by having a draughtsman handle the work between the artist and the designer. Bruegel condensed the process by being artist-draughtsman-

85.
LUCAS VAN LEYDEN,
The Dance of the Madgalene.
Engraving, 1519.

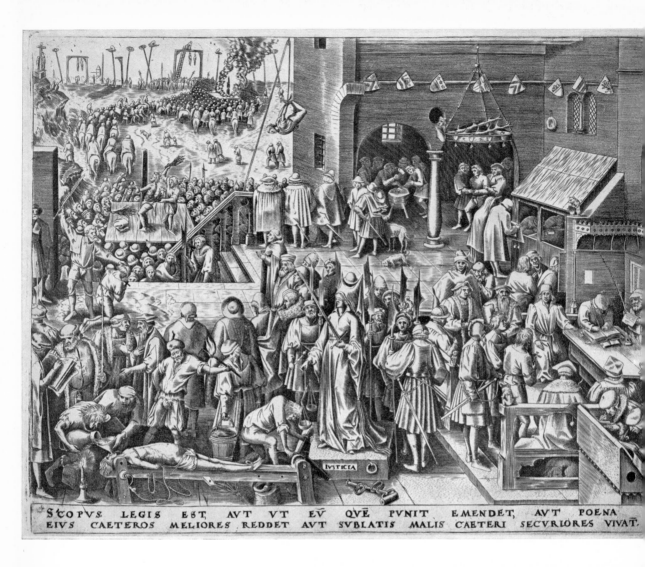

SCOPVS. LEGIS EST, AVT VT EV QVE PVNIT EMENDET, AVT POENA
EIVS CAETEROS MELIORES REDDET AVT SVBLATIS MALIS CAETERI SECVRIORES VIVAT.

86.

PIETER BRUEGEL, THE ELDER,
c. 1525-1569,
Justice.
Engraving, 1559.

87.

PIETER BRUEGEL, THE ELDER,
The Rich Kitchen.
Engraving, 1563.

Ou Maigre-os Le pot mouue est vu pouure Conuiue   Daer maghermau die pot roert is een arm ghasterije
Pourre, à Graſſe-cuiſine iray, tant que ie Vrue   aus Loop irk nae de vette Querken met herfen bije

88.

PIETER BRUEGEL, THE ELDER,
The Poor Kitchen.
Engraving, 1563.

89.

PIETER BRUEGEL, THE ELDER,
The Alchemist.
Engraving, 1558.

designer in one operation. His drawings for Cock have been compared to blueprints for the engraver's work. He thus maintained a higher than usual degree of control over the final product signed with his name.

Bruegel did hundreds of engravings for Cock and it seems clear that he reversed the usual relationship: many of the paintings he did later were based on designs first conceived and executed at the old firm. He traveled to Italy and was one of the earliest artists to be impressed more by the Italian landscape than by Italian art. He did landscapes for Cock, often under a religious title and with tiny figures of *Magdalene in Repentence* or *St. Anthony in the Desert* buried in the wide-screen vista of mountains, plains, and rivers. He did a series of vessels, a kind of maritime Who's Who, comparable, perhaps, to *Jane's Fighting Ships.* But Bruegel's ships, cockleshells by today's nautical standards, have still the power to evoke the feeling of wind on the sea and sensitive ships handled by masters.

In his engravings, as later in his painting, Bruegel became an early user of the common people and their ways as material fit for art. The costumes and gestures of the festivals of fools and the rowdy country dances are depicted and sometimes transmuted into the scenery of a supernatural hellish world akin to that invented earlier by Bruegel's countryman, Bosch. A point of view emerged in the work of the faithful creator of scenes and ships. In a series of prints on the Seven Virtues, Bruegel came to *Justice,* and the realistic eye and hand depicted no ideal scene of the goddess of right relations, but rather the legal violence that was practiced in Flanders and everywhere else, in Bruegel's time and long afterwards, in the name of Justice. In the foreground a man is stretched on the rack and another is pushed in to an inquisitorial court. In the middle distance, a poor wretch is flogged as a public exhibition, a man is trussed and swung high, and a prisoner, presumably a thief, has his hand cut off. On the horizon, the condemned are exposed on high wheels; others are hung on the gallows; and one victim burns at the stake. In the center, Justice herself, blindfolded and equipped with scales and sword, is surrounded by armed men.

Here as in most of his work, Bruegel gained much by the sheer multiplication of detail. The contrast between *The Rich Kitchen* and *The Poor Kitchen* and the respective attitudes toward the unexpected guest could be banal, but Bruegel raised his contrast to effectiveness by making everything in the one so skinny and bare, in the other so plump and gross. Even the knives of the well-fed are fat; even the pots of the poor manage to seem thin.

Detail, too, is the heart of *The Alchemist,* with its thoroughgoing

Iulius, Augustus, nec non et Iunius Aestas.   AESTAS   Frugiferas aruis fert Aestas torrida meßeis.
Adoles _____ rentiæ imago.
m:i.s.

90.
PIETER BRUEGEL, THE ELDER,
Summer.
Engraving, 1568.

attack on self-seeking science which ends, as seen out the window, with the alchemist and his family asking a meal from the monks.

Bruegel used to dress as a peasant and spend time in the country getting to know the workers of the land. This practice never more completely justified itself than in *Summer*, from a suite of the Seasons. The bulky bodies that somehow move with grace and precision became a Bruegel characteristic in his painting. Here, as the printman turns his democratic instincts into art, those bodies come out of the distance to culminate in the great reaper who pauses to take a swig from the jug. The sun, itself, in its rays, repeats the movement of the reapers from far to near, and, in the mellow light, all of Bruegel's Flanders becomes more apt for art than any goddess.

The new system of print publishing worked like a charm for Bruegel. He was a fluke. Let us admit at once the system was designed to produce hacks and hackwork; it did produce hacks and hackwork in ever increasing quantities until, having gone through many changes, the system underwent its final change and vanished at the click of a camera's shutter.

In the centuries in between that beginning and that end, the system passed over some remarkable talent. One of the earliest examples was Hercules Seghers, a Dutchman born in the last years of the sixteenth century. The system used etching as an aid to engraving. Seghers was one of the first artists to make art out of etching itself. He experimented widely, especially in a limited use of color, based on using tinted papers or cloths as a printing surface. He also used drypoint for textural effects. Almost no two prints of any of his work are alike.

The importance of Seghers, however, is not really based on his technical advances. In using etching as a thing in itself, he discovered a new look for landscape and still life, a look of intensity and brooding that extended, for the first time, the human responses of the printmaker to the nonhuman world. Seghers' work was useless to the system. He printed his etchings himself and didn't sell many. After a life of poverty he died, it is said, from a fall while drunk. Among the few purchasers of his prints, apparently, was a young Amsterdam artist destined to create the finest etchings ever made, and to die, like Seghers, a complete financial failure. His name was Rembrandt van Rijn.

91.
HERCULES SEGHERS, 1589-c. 1640,
The Lamentation of Christ.
Etching, 1633-38.

Chapter Six

Rembrandt

Rembrandt

The story of Rembrandt's life and hard times is widely known; that's no reason not to tell it again. From one point of view, the poor man's life has been more influential than his art. There can't be a dozen artists in the world today really striving for the same total mastery of their art in either painting or prints; scarcely more share his faith in drawing. But what is conceived to be the moral lesson of Rembrandt's life is the faith of thousands.

The lesson is simple enough: Rembrandt died broke, unappreciated by his time because he was trying to do something new in art. Some years before his death his financial straits were so desperate he was forced into bankruptcy, he had his goods and chattels sold out from under him, and his entire artistic production was placed in the legal control of his mistress and his son. Within decades of his death the rehabilitation of Rembrandt began and ever since he has been thought one of the truly great. Moral: nothing succeeds like failure.

Remaining a failure, however, has become a difficult thing for an artist. Others have read the lesson of Rembrandt, too, among them many private purchasers of art and all museums and foundations. Today many a young artist concocts a solidly impenetrable manner only to find himself collected avidly, purchased by the Metropolitan, given a one-man show by the Museum of Modern Art, and packed off to Europe by the Guggenheim Foundation, there to meditate on the frustrations of being understood.

Both aspects of this interesting situation – the artists' determination to be unappreciated, and their public's determination to appreciate everything – derive ultimately from the ruin of Rembrandt, although both gained great strength from the somewhat later ruin of Rembrandt's countryman, Van Gogh. It is just possible, however, that this whole form-giving structure of contemporary art is based on a misreading of Rembrandt's ruin.

To begin with, bankruptcy is not entered into by the totally and permanently destitute. It results from an overextension of credit and expresses both the desire of the creditors to recover what they can from their debtor's existing capital, and the desire of the debtor to salvage what he can of the same capital. Credit, extended or overextended, implies a reasonable prospect of payment and hence the existence of a market for the goods or services of the debtor. For Rembrandt to get himself into bankruptcy at all, he had to be at least moderately successful, in order to have credit to overextend, and successful for a long enough time to acquire the nonliquid capital that would make the bankruptcy worthwhile. Such was the case.

Rembrandt was widely and deeply appreciated during his life and from an early age. His financial failure came from his own deliberate withdrawal from a brilliant career as a fashionable portrait

92.

REMBRANDT VAN RIJN, 1606-1669,
The Return of the Prodigal Son.
Etching, 1636.

artist, and from his own spectacular mismanagement of his money. Insofar as the society of seventeenth-century Amsterdam bears any responsibility for the artist's ruin, that responsibility comes not from a failure to appreciate, but from a too facile appreciation. Rembrandt, from the time he was in his mid-twenties, enjoyed the full favor of fashion and the high pay that goes with the job. He happened to be a great artist and passed beyond fashion in his work at about the same time that fashion, inevitably, was turning elsewhere. He lived, however, as if he planned to be fashionable forever. He made imprudent investments, bought a luxurious house which became a huge burden, and poured his money into art collecting.

Beyond the obvious truth that estate management is a specialized trade, the lesson to be taken from Rembrandt's ruin is that, in anything more substantial than dressmaking or automobile manufacture, fashion is folly. Nothing can be done to discourage the operation of fashion in art, but the astonishing thing about the reparations-to-Rembrandt movement is that it places cultural institutions of immense dignity at the total service of fashion, for all the world as if they were General Motors.

Rembrandt's international fame, from his youth until a few decades ago, was based chiefly on his etchings. His approach to printmaking was radically different from that of his peers among painters, Raphael and Rubens. Raphael, through the engraver, Raimondi, and Rubens, through a well-organized workshop, both set up efficient businesses for the exploitation of their paintings. The print operation for both was rather like a road company of a Broadway hit. In Raimondi's shop and even more in Rubens' this led to a high degree of standardization of line both for the purpose of "translating" paintings into prints and for the ensuring of the largest possible edition.

Both purposes were foreign to Rembrandt's print practice. Etching was for him an original art medium He used it in conjunction with other techniques, such as drypoint and *retroussage*, that made for small editions. He also came to make succeeding "states" of his prints. A "state" of a print is created by changing the plate after the printing of some impressions. Proofs taken in the course of working on a plate are obviously a help to the artist, but in Rembrandt's work the existence of several states also reveals a genuine deepening of the original artistic vision. The change is sometimes quite radical, as in the different states reproduced of *Christ Presented to the People* and the *Three Crosses*.

With the almost solitary exception of Seghers, etching before Rembrandt's time was used as a fast way of making engravings. The artist drew his lines – or, more often, the craftsman drew them according to the artist's design – upon the acid-resistant

93.
REMBRANDT VAN RIJN,
The Angel Appearing to the Shepherds.
Etching, 1634.

ground laid over the copper and the acid simply did the work conventionally done by the engraver's strength and skill and cutting edge. The etched lines could be and were strengthened by subsequent engraving in the lines, as a pencil sketch may be traced over in ink. The result of such etching was to destroy the peculiar character engraving derives from the resistance of copper to the cutting edge, and, at the same time, to leave unexplored the new technical and expressive possibilities of etching.

That exploration, Rembrandt made his own. The two outstanding new possibilities of etching that Rembrandt made into infinitely delicate instruments of expression were the increased directness of working on the plate, and the greatly extended range of light and dark. The first comes from the ease with which the etcher's needle moves through its ground; the second from the gradations possible by controlling the time various portions of the exposed copper are subject to the corrosive acid. Drypoint and its rich burr add to both effects.

Rembrandt was not the last religious artist, but he was in the last generation in which it was possible for great artists to find in Christianity thematic material for their complete engagement intellectually and complete fulfillment artistically. Among his contemporaries were Rubens, rather older, in Flanders, and Zurbaran and Velazquez in Spain. In the Catholic countries the strong impulse of the Counter Reformation gave a renewed and prolonged life to religious art, but that life expired as the impulse hardened into the fanaticism of the religious war. In Protestant Holland the situation of religious art was more complicated. There was a basic Puritanical suspicion of church art; this, combined with a rising class of entrepreneurial bourgeois, created conditions favorable to portrait, still-life and landscape painting. On the other hand, aided by Holland's successful war of independence against Spain and by the great growth of Netherlands wealth, there was a widespread feeling that the Dutch were really the Chosen People of God; this led to some interest in paintings and prints of Old Testament scenes, wherein the proto-Dutch of Palestine defied their enemies and carried out their mission. Like other aspects of Puritanism, this belief in one's own election by God turned up shortly in New England, but was not accompanied by much in the line of art.

Against that background of changing religious patterns in Europe, with the new pattern leading to the complete separation of church and art, Rembrandt created a new artistic embodiment of Europe's Christian faith. His new religious art was intensely personal in all the ways that word is used of an artist. His etchings of the traditional Gospel subjects present a view of the sacred persons and events in which the personality of the viewer, led by the personality of the artist, is brought into intimate contact with the

94.

REMBRANDT VAN RIJN,
The Three Trees.
Etching, 1643.

95.

REMBRANDT VAN RIJN,
Goldweigher's Field.
Etching, 1651.

sacred persons and their situations. The relative informality of the etched line may be cited as making this possible: it expresses so clearly the movement of the artist's hand holding the needle. Rembrandt's own religious faith can as readily be cited as impelling his mastery of the delicate means of etching.

For that faith, as seen in the etchings, is quite different from the faith expressed in the religious art of his contemporaries and predecessors. Rembrandt's is based upon a deep understanding and sympathy for the person of Jesus. There is, in complete humility, something of an identification between the artist and the Jesus of the prints. This is a radical change from the public religious art of the Italians, the Spanish, and the Flemish. The basic religious relationship is not that of the Catholics, between the individual and the Church, nor that of the Protestants, between the individual and the community of the Elect. Rather, it is between the individual and Jesus as presented in the Gospel. The greatest of Rembrandt's religious etchings are not representations of events, but profound commentaries on them, expressing the personal religious experience of a sensitive, devout mind.

The sensitive line reflecting that mind appears from the first in the little selfportraits that Rembrandt etched. Variations of clothing are tried, variations of expression. Constant is the inquiring gaze of the soul into itself. The early etchings of the artist's mother combine complete realism with deep affection.

Two religious prints made in Rembrandt's early years of prosperity contrast the two general methods he was exploring to make etching yield its expressive posibilities. *The Return of the Prodigal Son* is all line, although the lines here and there come close together. The scratching of the needle picks out the gaunt, angular and exhausted form of the youth, the heartbroken compassion of the father. The whole house – architecturally as well as in the persons of the family – comes down to meet the boy. The postures and gestures distinguish clearly and subtly among the degrees of welcome. The basic movement down, meeting the boy's desperate imploring, is softly strengthened by the planes of the house – solidly established in so few lines – meeting with the ascent of the steps. The very angle of the wanderer's staff plays its part in the expressive structure of the total group. Through the archway, the faintest of lines – drawn as if upon the air – suggests the dust of the road and the heat of the journey home. The parable of the prodigal son, related in the New Testament as an analogy of the kingdom of heaven, has been made an intensely human drama of repentance and forgiveness.

In *The Angel Appearing to the Shepherds*, the whole emotional and intellectual burden of the print is carried not by line but by the sharp contrast between light and dark and by the subtle shifting through the degrees of one or the other. There are two great

96.
REMBRANDT VAN RIJN,
Faust in his Study.
Etching, c. 1652-53.

centers of light, the angels on high and the shepherds below, who are hearing the news of Christ's birth. Between the two flows a deep gulf of dark, almost like an impassable river from the upper right to the lower left of the print. The point of the incident, in Rembrandt's view as in that of most Christians, is that the gulf between man and God, impassable for theological and historical reasons, has been bridged by the appearance of the angels over Bethlehem and the tidings they brought to mankind.

Within that dark gulf may be dimly seen a landscape of the earth, with light faintly glowing along hills, trees, a town and a river spanned by a bridge. As those forms exist within the darkness, so the angelic forms exist within the light. The two poles of light in the print are by no means equal. It is quite clear that the light on the shepherds, although it frightens them and their flocks, is a faint projection from the heavenly light of the angels. Shepherds and beasts are visible in part by the shadows upon them. The angels are light, becoming more clearly differentiated as they move toward the earth, less as they move toward the light. The faint lines in the very center of the light suggest swarms of cherubim emerging from absolute light as the town and the river emerge from pitch dark.

The angels tumbling out of light reach a climax of visibility and are fixed in the figure of the foremost angel, standing on a cloud and addressing the shepherds. The shepherds, scattering from the unexpected light, are climaxed in the shepherd, who, though frightened, does not run. The bodies of the animals express varieties of confusion: some bolt, some are fixed in their tracks. This is intensified in the reactions of the men. One runs blindly away. One falls on his back, overcome. Two look on, transfixed. The central shepherd is their focal point. He and the announcing angel are two poles between which leaps the spark of God's news for man.

Landscape, all but lost in the *Angels Appearing*, is the whole subject in two of Rembrandt's finest etchings. In an age when, as ever since, a landscape was relatively sure-fire, Rembrandt etched very few of them. Out of a total production of about three hundred prints, there are less than thirty landscapes. In most of them he went beyond the faithful reproduction of scene.

The Three Trees is based on the same dramatic play of light against dark and dark against light as the *Angels Appearing*. The trees are a dark mass against the sky. The light of the sky is cut in on along the top, to some extent in the upper right and most strongly in the sharp slanting lines on the left, in order to shape the light to fit the dark at its center. Yet neither light sky nor dark trees is stark. From the almost total darkness of the small triangular area in the upper left corner, the sky gets progressively lighter as it gets nearer the trees, yet it is never free of lines. The trees, so dark against the white sky, are nevertheless full of the

97.
REMBRANDT VAN RIJN,
Flight into Egypt.
Etching, 1654.

98.
REMBRANDT VAN RIJN,
*Christ Seated, Disputing
with the Doctors.*
Etching, 1630.

play of light and shadow within their silhouettes. This is true also of the dark bank on which the trees stand. The light of the sky is continued in the bit of reflection in the foreground stream and then is used as land light as the artist, with few lines and an amazing sense of graduated distance, takes us across the whole flat land of Holland.

The flatness and stretch of the land beneath the infinity of sky are even more magnificently shown in *The Goldweigher's Field*. The light and dark contrast is very subtle, much of it coming from the expert use of drypoint. The lines, delicate but strong, pick out a host of details which, when you look at them, become houses, ditches, peasants at work, and, when you don't, are simply part of the terrain sweep of Holland.

Faust in His Study deploys the light and dark of the etched plate around a central activity of Rembrandt's life, the pursuit of truth through the practice of an art. The legend of Faust, as swaggered by Marlowe and intoned by Goethe, is far from the tense quiet of the scholar's room. This Faust is not after his lost youth, nor does he seek a peep show of history. He wants the secret behind life and we see him at a moment of illumination. He rises from his chair, his hand still holding what could be the instrument of either scholar or printmaker. The magical disk glows against the light of all outdoors and makes the sunlight through the window seem dim. Even paler is the light on the celestial globe in the lower right. The living light, given its quality from the repeated but irregular lines with which it is broken, glows in two places: the disk and its radiance, and the face and form of Faust. The intensity of light is raised by the richly textured darkness. Quartered at the center of the disk are four letters from an occasion in which Rembrandt himself, in the pursuit of his art, was to find a measure of truth. They are the INRI that Pilate placed above the head of the dying Christ.

Rembrandt's small etchings of the childhood of Jesus are done without the dramatic contrast of light and dark that so dazzles in the *Angels Appearing to the Shepherds*. The three plates here reproduced are all much more even in tone. Yet within that narrower range there is all the contrast needed to carry Rembrandt's thought and feeling about the childhood of Jesus.

In *The Flight into Egypt*, the relatively heavy, coarse lines depict the little family fleeing from the hatred of Herod, the Palestinian puppet king determined to kill the child prophesied as "king." The thick lines do indeed convey the visual and tactile qualities of homespun cloth on Joseph, the foliage overhead, the rough coat of the donkey. Spaced farther apart, the lines are used for shadow on the mantle and cloak of Mary; spaced nearer together, they coalesce into the dark forest behind the travelers. Yet the roughness of the lines has in it also something of the roughness of the

99.

REMBRANDT VAN RIJN,
Christ between his Parents,
Returning from the Temple.
Etching, 1654.

journey: the abrupt departure, the weary road, the uncomfortable conditions, the fatigue and the danger behind. This is not to suggest the use of a deliberate symbolic language of line, only that the mind and heart have equal share with the eye and hand in controlling the point upon the copper.

Certainly the line is quite different in the *Christ Seated Disputing with the Doctors*. Massed lines are used mainly for shadow. The figures, especially those of Christ and the principal "doctors" are chiefly conveyed by outline and all lines are more delicate. There is variety of response in the faces of those listening but the responses suggested are all within a limited range. The focus is on the face and form of the boy Jesus. His sweet gravity is summed up in a few lines and the unique moment is characterized by the earnest gesture of the hand and the boyish swing of the right leg. The event is the single emergence of Jesus from the so-called "hidden life" led at Nazareth. The family had gone up to Jerusalem for Passover. Joseph and Mary missed Jesus on the return trip with a group of pilgrims. They returned to the capital and found him, according to St. Luke, "in the temple, sitting in the midst of the doctors, hearing them and asking them questions." *Christ Between His Parents, Returning from the Temple* follows that incident. The tone of the lines to some extent combines that of the other two. The background, darkening foliage in the first, the flat wall of the temple in the second, open now to the hilly Judean landscape. There is a left to right progression within the background from near to far and from dark to light. As in the *Goldweigher's Field*, the terrain reveals, on examination, houses, a village, a pool of water, men and animals, all blended into the landscape on first glance. Returning to Nazareth, Jesus explained, "I must be about my Father's business," but nevertheless he accompanied Mary and Joseph to the small town where he lived for more than a decade and a half before he began the public ministry. The curve of the background suggests abstractly something of that situation, but it exists at its most powerful in the aspiration of the boy's face between the submission of Mary and the patient humility of Joseph. The textural difference between the shadows on Mary's garments and those on Joseph's seems similarity beside the contrasting white of Jesus.

In dealing with the preaching ministry of Christ, Rembrandt created what is beyond doubt the most famous etching and quite likely the most famous and best loved print in existence. *Christ Healing the Sick* (the "Hundred Guilder Print") combines several incidents in the Gospels. The lame and the blind are led, carried, and wheeled. The poor have the Gospel preached to them and the children are welcomed. In the shadow of the city wall of Jerusalem, Christ preaches, the light goes forth into the darkness, and the whole composition moves from both sides to the preacher.

100.

REMBRANDT VAN RIJN,
Christ Healing the Sick.
Etching and dry-point, 2nd state, c. 1642-45.

Nearest him are the poor and oppressed, who approach him in hope and trust. On the left, as in the print of the boy in the temple, the faces register the degrees of skeptical response. On the right, apparently in the gate known as the "Needle's Eye," a camel has difficulty getting through; the beast's master wears the turban of a "rich man," who, according to Christ, has similar difficulty entering the kingdom of heaven. The face of Jesus shines with patience and love in the midst of the people he has come to save and the forces that will destroy him.

The destruction is accomplished in *The Three Crosses.* The print exists in numerous states, two of which are reproduced. The changes are the most drastic ever introduced in a print scene that remains essentially the same from state to state. The light changes radically. Characters vanish, others appear. Christ on the cross remains constant, but to look from the early state to the later is to watch the body grow emaciated and approach death. The overall light darkens, as a result of which the light behind Christ's head and down his body takes on a different quality, as if it came from within.

It has been suggested that in executing and printing the succeeding states, Rembrandt intended a series on the Crucifixion. It may have been. The prints themselves speak powerfully of an ever more deeply realized conviction, taking its progress in the act of working on the plate.

The other celebrated example of Rembrandt's changing his basic image as the plate passed from state to state is the *Christ Presented to the People.* The moment is Pilate's "presentation" of the beaten-up victim to the crowd in the hope that the visible evidence of punishment will placate those who demanded the death sentence. The changes from the early state to the later are all directed toward the same end. There are some architectural changes, the combined effect of which is to move the whole tableau slightly forward, nearer the viewer. Lines have been added everywhere and earlier lines have been further etched, so that both darkness and solidity have come upon the buildings. In the early state, the whole building half-resembles a stage set; in the later, it bears down with the weight of masonry upon the victim presented and upon the spectator. The victim himself has grown more pitiable, more abject. Pilate, from the sympathetic evasion of the early state, has passed into grossness.

The most remarkable change, however, is in the lower third of the plate. Not only the crowd but the very ground it stood on has been taken away. Instead a black gulf, punctuated by the arches of the platform, yawns before the artist and the viewer alike. We are no longer watching a simple historical event, Rembrandt makes clear. We are taking part in one. Christ, beaten and passive, is "presented" not to a Judean crowd of the first

101.

REMBRANDT VAN RIJN,
The Three Crosses.
Etching, 1st state, 1653.

102.

REMBRANDT VAN RIJN,
The Three Crosses.
Etching, 4th state, 1653.

century, but to a Dutch individual of the seventeenth, and to those who have come since then to the print.

Rembrandt himself, in his later years, faced such a "presentation" as he pictured for Christ. The crowd of admirers and patrons melted away and the artist found himself presented to a void. In that void he kept working and kept faith with his own pursuit of truth. His celebrated bankruptcy had little effect on his production, although prints declined as he concentrated more and more on the luminous reality of his paintings. Death took Hendrickje, the support and inspiration of his old age, and Rembrandt worked on. Then his only surviving son, Titus, died. The darkness which the artist had created, fought, and shaped so often to his own purposes, was taking more and more of the artist's life. The following year, 1669, the darkness was complete when Rembrandt died at sixty-three, stripped of the furnishings and the persons who had made his world but left, to the end, with the inner light that gave that world its meaning.

After Rembrandt, the religious print, and indeed religious art in all forms, was no longer an enterprise for the serious artist. When, after more than two centuries, artists returned to Judaeo-Christianity for material, they returned to the personal, lonely encounter with religious truth, the mode of Rembrandt.

103.

REMBRANDT VAN RIJN,
Christ Presented to the People.
Etching, 1st state, 1655.

104.

REMBRANDT VAN RIJN,
Christ Presented to the People.
Etching, 7th state, 1655.

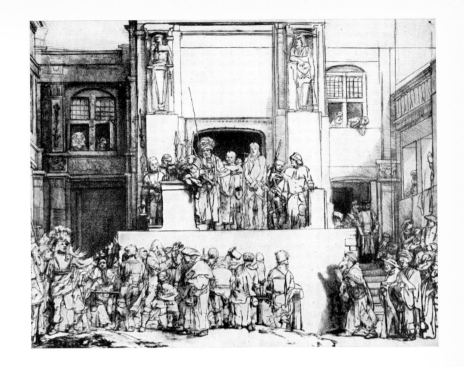

Two Professionals, Callot and Piranesi

Two Professionals, Callot and Piranesi

In the nineteenth century, collectors of etchings made a sharp distinction between the "professional" and the "amateur" of the art. In the hands of the amateur, etching was presumed to be at least available for the higher purposes of art. The professional, on the other hand, was presumed to be automatically a vulgarizer and without merit. The professional engaged his services to popular piety, to tourism or to the illustration of contemporary history. The amateur alone could afford to be interested in art.

This view of the relative merits of the amateur and the professional is without parallel except in the fields of politics and sex, where similar views are held for similar reasons.

In printmaking, at least, this view has a good deal to recommend it. The most professional of professionals, from the sixteenth century to the beginning of the twentieth, were largely preoccupied with trying to do laboriously by hand what today is done so flawlessly by the camera and the various photo-mechanical printing processes. The imitation of nature was only part, and not the major part, of the professional preoccupation. More important for the business of printmaking was the perfecting of a cheap method which would yield impressions always the same in the highest possible number. Eventually this quest led to steel-facing for the relatively soft copper of the etched plate. Long before that, however, in both etching and engraving, the professionals developed systems of parallel or intersecting lines, the chief function of which was to last a long time in printing.

These regular lines act as a mechanical screen between the eye and the object perceived. The effect is as if a fishnet were thrown over a form and the draughtsman then drew not the form but the curves of the net caused by the presence of the form. The ultimate refinement of this technique is banknote engraving. The portrait of Washington on a one-dollar bill reveals, even to the unassisted eye, the net of lines that the engraver has, in effect, thrown over the head and shoulders of the President in order to reveal their contours.

The contours are revealed, but the net is a screen. The word "screen" is used to describe the immeasurably finer system of dots used to print photographs in halftone reproduction. Any newspaper photo will reveal, under a magnifying glass, the regular system on which it is based and which permits the printing of millions of impressions in a few hours. The important differences between the halftone screen and the screens devised by etchers and engravers are these: The halftone screen is so fine that it becomes practically invisible, a state never approached by the older screens; the halftone screen takes care of itself and need not concern the photographer, while the screen was a chief preoccupation of the old printmaker; in reproducing fine art, the halftone screen permits the following of a system of lines and

Cicho Sgarra. Collo Francisco.

Gian Fritello. Ciurlo.

Cap. Spessa Monti. BaGattino.

Cap. Bonbardon. Cap. Grillo.

Cap. Esgangarato. Cap. Cocodrillo.

Taglia Cantoni. Fracasso.

105-110.
JACQUES CALLOT, 1592-1635,
Balli di Sfessania.
Etchings, 1621.

111.

JACQUES CALLOT,
Beggar on Crutches.
Etching, 1622.

112.

JACQUES CALLOT,
A Suffering Beggar Seated.
Etching, 1622.

16

15

113-120.

JACQUES CALLOT,
The Gobbi:
Title Page,
The Flageolet Player,
The Drinker,
The Mandolin Player,
Hunchback with Cane,
The Drinker Dancing,
Hunchback Seen from Behind,
Man with Big Hat.
Etchings, 1622.

VARIE FIGVRE GOBBI
di Iacopo Callot
fatto in firenza
l'anno 1616

excudit Nancij

lights by the original, while the older screens imposed their own system.

The last point brings up the fact that until the present century the vast majority of professional printmakers were "translators" of paintings and drawings created by other men. The printmaker's job was to reproduce someone else's original and unique creation in such a way that an image of the original could be had by many. It is for this reason that the connoisseurs and curators of the last century habitually used the terms painter-etcher and painter-engraver to distinguish the original artist in prints from the merely skillful copyist. The implication of both names was that the practitioner who was only an etcher or only an engraver was probably not much of an artist. Historically, the implication is largely correct. Most of the great names in prints are also great names in painting: Dürer, Holbein, Rembrandt, Goya, Hogarth, Daumier, Rouault. But there are exceptions, and furthermore the relationship between an artist's practice of painting and his practice of printmaking is infinitely varied.

Among the most strictly professional printmakers, from time to time the spark of originality combined with the gift of drawing to produce printed images with the ability to stretch the mind or to stir the heart of the observer. Two outstanding professionals whose work has such ability were Jacques Callot of the seventeenth century and Giovanni Battista Piranesi of the eighteenth. Neither was ever a painter and, while Piranesi had architectural ambitions, both men poured their whole artistic energy into printmaking.

Callot, indeed, has long been recognized as one of the most influential of printmakers. Etching techniques he developed were studied by Rembrandt and adapted to his own needs. Callot's influence was more widespread, however, among the reproductive printmakers. He invented or perfected various ways in which etching could be made to get something of the elegance of engraving, notably by the use of the *échoppe*, which, used in place of a conventional etcher's needle, permits the drawing of the line, typical of engraving, that swells and diminishes from center to end.

Callot, a native of Lorraine, received early training as a goldsmith. Following the migration of a boyhood friend, Callot went to Rome at the age of sixteen. There he apprenticed himself to an engraver and got his big break when a rush job came through from the Medici rulers of Florence. Young Callot delivered the order, stayed on to complete it and presently found himself, along with Galileo, the recipient of Medici patronage. He received room and board and a studio in the Uffizi, now one of the great art museums of the world, but then still the "office building" of the Medici court. For the Medici, Callot engraved and etched

121.
JACQUES CALLOT,
The Temptation of St. Anthony.
Etching, 1634.

subjects setting forth the victories and virtues of members of the family. He memorialized the outdoor fêtes and entertainments given in the public squares. He illustrated a news report of sea battles against the Turks off the coast of Genoa.

The Medici had become rulers of Florence and patrons of the arts primarily because of their fifteenth-century success as bankers and merchants. In the early seventeenth century, Callot's patron, the Grand Duke Cosimo II, took the family out of trade, thus giving the Medici the aristocratic authenticity they had never needed in the days of their greatness, and in the process drastically reducing the family income. When Cosimo died, the Grand Duchy had to economize. Callot was laid off.

Back in his native Nancy, capital of Lorraine, Callot discovered that if the Medici weren't like the Medici anymore, neither was anyone else. He picked up a few jobs designing for fêtes but there wasn't much patronage in the provincial capital and none at all of the disinterested kind he had enjoyed in Florence. Callot reworked some of his earlier plates for public sale and created several new series of small figures, based chiefly on his experience in Italy of the peculiarly Italian theatrical form, the Commedia dell'Arte. In Callot's time, the early seventeenth century, the Commedia was nearing the end of its run, a run which lasted hundreds and perhaps thousands of years. In that same seventeenth century Molière was to make dramatic literature out of Commedia plots, situations and characters; in France, through Molière, the vagabond group of low-life actors became the Comédie Française, a far cry from sleeping in fields and performing in village squares.

The Commedia that Callot knew in Italy had enjoyed great prosperity for some two hundred years and had its own well-established language of gesture, pantomime, and dance. The plots were simple, often concerned with marriage, with swindles of various kinds, or with the adventures of such types as the miser, the seducer or the braggart soldier. The doctor, with his fearsome syringe, was a stock source of humor. The Commedia was as close to "pure" theater as history has known. There were no scripts. The story was tacked up on the side of the stage. The actors read the script and improvised their lines as they went along, inserting their acrobatic specialties where suitable.

This is the theater recorded by Callot in his series of *Italian Comedians*, the *Balli di Sfessania*. It is as futile to study one of these characters in isolation as it would be to excerpt a soliloquy from the Italian players. Callot presents his players in pairs and the eye should move rapidly from pair to pair. The life and movement, the grotesque exaggeration, the sense of insult as an art form, and the sense – all but vanished from the stage today – of sex as a comic aberration – all this dances through the etched

122-127.

JACQUES CALLOT,
The Little Miseries:
The Camp,
Pillaging a Monastery,
Attacking Travelers on the Highway,
Ravaging and Burning a Village,
Peasants Take Revenge on Soldiers,
The Hospital.
Etchings, 1633-35.

128.

JACQUES CALLOT,
The Miseries and Disasters of War:
Frontispiece.
Etching, 1633.

129.

JACQUES CALLOT,
The Miseries and Disasters of War:
Enrolling the Troop.
Etching.

30.
JACQUES CALLOT,
*The Miseries and Disasters of War:
The Battle.*
Etching.

31.
JACQUES CALLOT,
*The Miseries and Disasters of War:
The Marauders.*
Etching.

32.
JACQUES CALLOT,
*The Miseries and Disasters of War:
Pillage of a House.*
Etching.

33.
JACQUES CALLOT,
*The Miseries and Disasters of War:
Devastation of a Monastery.*
Etching.

134.

JACQUES CALLOT,
*The Miseries and Disasters of War:
Firing the Village.*
Etching.

135.

JACQUES CALLOT,
*The Miseries and Disasters of War:
Attack on the Wagon.*
Etching.

136.

JACQUES CALLOT,
*The Miseries and Disasters of War:
Catching the Marauders.*
Etching.

137.

JACQUES CALLOT,
*The Miseries and Disasters of War:
The Strappado.*
Etching.

138.

JACQUES CALLOT,
The Miseries and Disasters of War:
The Hangman's Tree.
Etching.

139.

JACQUES CALLOT,
The Miseries and Disasters of War:
A Firing Squad of Arquebusiers.
Etching.

140.

JACQUES CALLOT,
The Miseries and Disasters of War:
The Slaughter.
Etching.

141.

JACQUES CALLOT,
The Miseries and Disasters of War:
Breaking on the Wheel.
Etching.

lines of the little figures. Taken in sequence, this parade of pairs gives precisely the feeling of Molière's own variations on the Comedians, those fast scenes in which two characters elaborate without repetition their respective comments like two perfectly matched tennis players.

Also while at Nancy, Callot did a series of *Beggars* and a series of *Gobbi* – dwarfs and hunchbacks – based on his Italian sketches. The *Beggars* strike a note of sober observation. The *Gobbi* seem as if the human victims of the beggars have been absorbed into the stylized distortion of the Commedia.

All this interest in the grotesque in art and life was accompanied by increasing numbers of straightforward, journeyman representations of Lorraine nobles and of local fêtes, the printman serving the function at such gatherings that the picture-magazine photographer serves today. All through Callot's adult life the Thirty Years' War was being waged and he picked up several commissions commemorating French and Spanish victories, the most notable being the Siege of Breda. This work gave the etcher a professional acquaintance with the armies whose presence characterized his time. Callot's evident delight in the grotesque received its supreme expression in a *Temptation of St. Anthony*, executed the year before the artist died. As a picture of the forces of hell, Callot's certainly presents the triumph of the Commedia over the Comedy called Divine. Anthony is lost in the clouds of demons and their practical jokes. The composition has a stage balance to it, with the four borders clearly forming the proscenium arch and the floor of some imaginary stage and the general spirit of most of the demons is that of the Commedia players.

At about the same time, Callot, in sinking health, had the subject he'd been waiting for brought home to him. The Duchy of Lorraine, during Callot's final years, had begun the process of losing its independence to Richelieu's France. The French invaded the province three times in an effort to keep it attached to the French plan for Europe. The third time saw the establishment of a French army of occupation, to remain there throughout Callot's life. The artist began work on which rests his lasting fame, *The Miseries of War*.

Callot's other great project having to do with the wars of his time, the *Siege of Breda*, was on a vast scale. Central to the theme was the arrival of the Spanish Infanta to take possession of the conquered town. The print was etched on six folio-size plates, their proofs to be pasted together into a single picture about four by five feet. In the *Miseries*, Callot reversed his scale, compressing into a few inches the burdens imposed by war on those who actually fought it and on those who get in the way.

He did the so-called *"Little Miseries"* first, a set of six plates, each only two by four and a half inches. The small set was not

142.

JACQUES CALLOT,
*The Miseries and Disasters of War:
The Wounded Seek Refuge
in a Hospital.*
Etching.

143.

JACQUES CALLOT,
*The Miseries and Disasters of War:
The Death on the Road.*
Etching.

144.

JACQUES CALLOT,
*The Miseries and Disasters of War:
Revenge of the Peasants.*
Etching.

145.

JACQUES CALLOT,
*The Miseries and Disasters of War:
Distribution of Wages.*
Etching.

printed until after Callot's death and he is said to have abandoned it to do the "large" set of eighteen, each just under three inches by just over seven. But the six stand by themselves as a swift-moving set of miseries observed. The soldiers are seen in camp, then they are practicing the ambuscade and free-lance hanging of robbed victims that were part of war. A church is looted and burned. The pillage and rapine spreads out from the church to an entire village. In the fifth plate the outraged peasants strike back at the soldiers, cutting them down with scythes and shooting them from hiding. The little set ends as does war, with the mutilated and ruined begging their bread and presenting petitions to those who have survived unscathed and who have even prospered from the wars.

Throughout the six, the entire effect is carried by the facts themselves and by Callot's judicious selection of just those particular facts. The settings are neutral and quiet. The soldiers, in their Baroque, seventeenth-century costumes, are accepted at the evaluation of their uniform maker; if anything, Callot even exaggerates the exaggerations of the clothes, giving the musketeers even more grace than they purchased with their plumed hats and ribboned boots.

The dry, non-editorializing presentation continues through the large set. Callot goes out of his way to start the military show with a semblance of its legality and proper functioning. The series opens with a recruiting scene and the soldiers drawn up in proper ranks. He also included a battle scene, where noble horsemen still wore the armor of another day. Soon, however, war gets down to its own business, which is neither splendid marching nor glorious battle, but chiefly the inflicting of misery upon humanity.

In the small set the miseries inflicted were mostly spontaneous and individual: banditry and rape are only rarely official policy. In the large set, the same kind of free enterprise continues, as in *The Marauders* and *The Pillage of a House*, but now these ventures by small groups take place within the frame of misery as policy. Devastation has been institutionalized. Thus the burning of the church in *Devastation of a Monastery* follows the small version closely, but significant changes relate the act to a larger and organized band of soldiers, rather than to the unorganized enthusiasm of a few. In the background, left, for instance, looting has become systematic; and the removal of the enthusiastic ax-swingers from the roof of the burning building has depersonalized the action.

Similarly in *The Maimed and Wounded Seek Refuge in a Hospital*, the mutilated and impoverished veterans in the larger set now have an organized open-air soup kitchen and present their petition in the shadow of the institutionalized Church: "Mother of Grace, Mother of Mercy," reads in part the Latin inscription.

146.

GIOVANNI BATTISTA PIRANESI,
1720-1778,
Arch of Titus.
Etching, c. 1760.

147.

GIOVANNI BATTISTA PIRANESI,
Hadrian's Villa,
the Central Room
of the Larger Thermae.
Etching, c. 1760.

More impressively still, the whole power of the state is brought to bear upon the tortured wretches who are the enemy. The army turns out on parade for executions. Men are hanged by the score; executioners operate in platoons. The state's Church offers the consolations of religion to the dying as part of the tableau. It is this matter-of-fact record that gives Callot his power. Everything is orderly, organized, and unthinkable. In the plates there is no hysteria, hardly any overt comment. These atrocities are simply part of war and war, as the world is organized in Callot's view, is inescapably part of life.

It took Callot almost the whole of his short life – he died in 1635 at the age of forty-three – to move in his work from professional support of the rulers of his age to intense criticism of their most characteristic institution, war. In the following century another professional printman began his career with such an inversion of professional purpose and allowed the inversion to influence a great many of the "straight" prints he created thereafter.

The man was Giovanni Battista Piranesi, an eighteenth-century Venetian who became the loyalest Roman of them all. Piranesi's trade was the making of prints of the monuments of Rome for tourists. His profession was architecture and he seems to have gone into printmaking originally as one way to practice architecture in the absence of any demand for him to build buldings. Beyond a trade and a profession, Piranesi also had a passion, the grandeur that was Rome. Indeed, he may have invented the grandeur that was Rome; at any rate the testimony of some notable eighteenth-century tourists says that Rome seemed far grander to them in Piranesi's prints than it did when they arrived on the spot. If Piranesi is thus to be considered the inventor of tourist illustration, a tradition of enlargement stronger today than ever, it is the least of his bequests to the two centuries that have succeeded his.

To the end of the eighteenth and early part of the nineteenth centuries, Piranesi contributed directly that Roman fever which became neoclassicism and which created, among other things, the city of Washington. In collaboration with the English architect Adam, Piranesi played an important part in the creation of the styles called Adam and Sheraton. The Italian also seems to be chiefly responsible for the Egyptian revival of the early nineteenth century. Since the Roman grandeurs Piranesi etched were necessarily ruins, with walls tumbled and foliage blooming on broken arches, his work was in part the inspiration of that curious English vogue for constructed ruins as landscape decorations. Prints began anticipating movie techniques at least as early as Holbein. Piranesi's contribution to what has been called the "grammar of the film" was the invention of the angle shot. Earlier

148.
GIOVANNI BATTISTA PIRANESI,
Appian Way Near Albano.
Etching, 1764.

Prospetto del Lastricato e de'margini dell'antica via Appia, delineato così come si vede verso Roma poco più in quà della città d'Albano.

149.
GIOVANNI BATTISTA PIRANESI,
The Prisons.
Etching, 1761.

150.
GIOVANNI BATTISTA PIRANESI,
The Prisons.
Etching, 1761.

151.
GIOVANNI BATTISTA PIRANESI,
The Prisons.
Etching, 1761.

Venetians, notably Tintoretto, had used an off-angle point of view in painting. Piranesi expanded and exploited the off-angle to its full range of dramatic effects. His predecessors in the Roman tourist print business were content to etch or engrave a straight-on view of whatever antiquity or curiosity they were presenting. Piranesi stood off to one side or the other, thus getting away from a blueprint type of elevation and automatically increasing the visual drama. He also anticipated the movies' use of the high angle and is said to have made some drawings suspended in a sling over the subject, rather as the camera is manipulated today – or was before the wide screen immobilized it.

The low-angle was actually Piranesi's favored point of view, since it increased the sweep and soar of the Roman grandeur. He also exploited the dramatizing effects of extreme light and dark contrasts. It is reported that he used to sketch a scene on copper in daylight for the main masses and textures, then finish the plate by moonlight for the sake of shadow.

All of these effects, dramatic and sometimes melodramatic, Piranesi brought into play in his masterpiece, the sixteen etchings of his imaginary *Prisons*. The *Prisons* are also Piranesi's gift to the twentieth century, in which man has not only rediscovered the fearsome instruments of torture that are scattered through these interiors, but especially discovered the more subtle tortures of the lost and aimless feeling that provides most of the weight for the great piers and beams of Piranesi's *Prisons*.

He etched the series first in 1745, when he was twenty-five, in light tones, on commission from a printseller. Sixteen years later Piranesi brought out his own set of *Prisons*, with two added plates, with everything darkened and strengthened and with the looming interiors everywhere broken up by wooden galleries, platforms, stairs, and even drawbridges. The title plate sets the tone. In the foreground, almost on top of us, is a torture wheel, yet the eye is compelled up, past the author's inscription, up, up until it is lost in space that has no end. At the same time, in the foreground, looming over the wheel and over us, is a masonry arch, pressing down on us. At the same time again, the grated opening in the lower left and the arch supporting the stair in the lower right suggest there are depths beneath us. Thus, Piranesi manages to have things all ways in order to increase the sense of diffident doom, a sense that permeates the *Prisons* and the work of twentieth-century writers as different as Kafka and Eliot.

The second plate, new to the 1761 edition, specifically refers to the Roman antiquities that were so much of Piranesi's life. There are ancient marbles and resurrected buildings and again the deliberate destruction of a precise location. We are both indoors and outdoors, at the bottom and yet with populated depths below

152.

GIOVANNI BATTISTA PIRANESI,
The Prisons.
Etching, 1761.

153.

GIOVANNI BATTISTA PIRANESI,
The Prisons.
Etching, 1761.

us. In the third plate, the figures dwindle to fleeting shadows along the stairs and platforms. The masonry takes over, shaping space and opening space after space. So it continues in the succeeding plates. We see a race of dwarfs, engaged in puny labor or bent on little missions inside the monstrous prisons of light and shade. Always the huge stone arches and walls are cluttered with wooden structures which, as often as not, lead nowhere, serve no purpose. Lanterns are dark and hang like the weight on a plumb line. The prison is a maze, a labyrinth in which imprisoned man meets restraint only on the endless stairs and in the shadows heavy as stone.

154.

GIOVANNI BATTISTA PIRANESI,
The Prisons.
Etching, 1761.

155.

GIOVANNI BATTISTA PIRANESI,
The Prisons.
Etching, 1761.

Hogarth

Hogarth

In the oldest section of New York City, the oldest establishment is Trinity Churchyard. For an hour or so in mid-morning and again in mid-afternoon, in the shadow of the church and the shade of the trees, the visitor can move placidly along the paths between the graves of the long dead. Yet half a block away the narrow streets are jammed with hustlers of every description and every level of age and fortune, intent to a man on the big dollar and the main chance. Something of that contrast is evident when you turn from Piranesi's *Prisons* to the London of William Hogarth.

Some such contrast existed in the cities themselves in the eighteenth century. Rome was dying once more, a role the city plays with the finesse of long practice; its next rebirth was a century in the future when Piranesi died. Throughout Hogarth's life, on the contrary, London was growing toward its world leadership. Swarming, brawling, boisterous, vulgar, the London crowd made the city streets a risk by day and a peril by night. Where there were crowds there were thieves, and the crowds were everywhere. Where there was darkness there was a band of brigands and cutthroats. Where there was a window there was a brimming pot to be emptied out of it. In Piranesi's Rome, as in his *Prisons* – if the two are really distinct – architecture has triumphed over the puny figures who flit like shadows down the great stairs and along the dead-end platforms. In Hogarth's London the buildings are often as flimsy and jerry-built as the carnival structures of *Southwark Fair*, barely able to contain the press of sweating, striving humanity.

Unable to do so, in fact, at Southwark: on the left, beneath the idealized advertisement of their show, the players tumble off their crude stage into the crowd. The contrast between painted representation is carried across the picture; all three structures are decked with posters; the poor players are nothing like so fine. The contrast continues in the crowd. A farmer on holiday has his pocket picked. A splendidly costumed warrior is served a summons for debt. Out of the roil emerge two figures in moments of genuine daring and skill. The rope dancer on the left, the steeple flyer on the right are part of it all, yet above it all, literally. Behind both, Hogarth shows the peaceful hills of the country around London and the gentle English sky above.

The thing that makes the print, however, is Hogarth's magnificent stroke in pulling the qualities of those distant hills and that glowing sky right into the central point of the picture, the lovely figure and abstracted face of the girl drummer. All across the picture runs the juxtaposition of sweaty reality with the hardly less vulgar dreams of the placard. Piercing this contrast is a third alternative, the fusion of dream and reality in the drummer girl and the distant hills.

Such a vision of a lovely English girl suddenly seen in the jostle

156.
WILLIAM HOGARTH, 1697-1764,
Southwark Fair.
Engraving, 1733.

of English noise recurs in Hogarth's engravings. Despite the title she is clearly the center of the *Enraged Musician*. The girl was given her definitive incarnation in Hogarth's finest painting, the *Shrimp Girl*.

The artist took his earliest training as a metal engraver but set himself up as a painter and printmaker at an early age. His hates were many – the "phiz-mongers" of British portraiture, the dealers in heavily varnished "black paintings" from Italy, the town gentry involved in continuing efforts to impose "correct taste" upon British art. Until Hogarth, the best British artists were all portrait painters and all foreigners. Holbein was one of them, Van Eyck another. Hogarth despised the French, chiefly, it seems, because they weren't English. To some extent he shared his countrymen's fears of the Jews and the Catholics, those inefficient conspirators who, even today, haven't much furthered their dark designs of conquest.

Both conspiracies are recorded in passing in *Humors of an Election Entertainment*, the first plate in *The Election* series. The candidates are feasting their constituents. Votes are bought for both money and love. Through the open window may be seen an effigy with a Levantine profile, hung with the sign, "No Jews!" This refers to a proposed bill of the fifties whereby immigrant Jews would be permitted to become British subjects. Britain was in danger and Britons rallied. On the floor is a paper, "Give us our eleven days." England had but recently joined Europe in using the two-hundred-year-old Gregorian calendar and the feeling was widespread that the Pope of Rome had somehow stolen eleven days from the lives of Englishmen. Again, as Hogarth reports, Britons rallied, but you can't win 'em all and the Englishmen never have got back their eleven days.

Hogarth made his name and his fortune with a series of six plates issued in 1732, *A Harlot's Progress*. The six engravings trace the swift rise and slow fall of a London whore, from her arrival in the capital to her death. As a pictorial dramatist, Hogarth was faced with the translation of time into space. Stage drama has time and sequence of speech and action. Hogarth, the dramatist, had none of these things. He got some time, of course, by making prints in series, but in itself this only gave him a sequence of tableaux. He extended the sequence by compressing different phases of his subject into single plates, while never seeming to, thus allowing the pictorial convention of a single, selected moment to remain unviolated.

In the first plate, *Moll Hackabout and Mother Needham*, the central subject, the moment of the scene, is Moll's arrival in the city and her encounter with Mother Needham, a notorious procuress. Mother Needham pats Moll's chin as one might a piece

THE ENRAGED MUSICIAN.

157.
WILLIAM HOGARTH,
Enraged Musician.
Engraving, 1741.

of poultry, say, the country goose, dead and delivered, which lies in Moll's basket.

From that moment of encounter, Hogarth stretches into the country past and the city future. To the left is the York wagon-coach on which Moll traveled and a country clergyman is astride a country plug. The girl has come up to enter service. The nature of the service is to the right. On the doorstep are Colonel Chartres, the master procurer of London who died before the time Hogarth engraved this series, and his pimp-in-waiting, John Gourlay. Their postures tell their relationship to each other and Chartres' features foretell Moll's future.

By the second plate that future has come with a rush. *Moll in Keeping* presupposes that, since we saw her last, the country girl has been citified, seduced, abandoned and, not only placed out to hire as mistress to a rich Jew — the conspiracy is on again — but even endowed with a clandestine lover of her own. The immediate past is clear enough from the lover's — and Moll's — dishabille as he tiptoes out the door while Moll creates a diversion by kicking over the tea table. Hogarth comments on his own compression of time by the "stop-action" position of the tilting teapot.

The wages of sin is further sin. Turned out by her protector, Moll, in plate three, has entered the retail end of the trade. The moment is breakfast, which she is served by her maid. Sitting in bed, Moll displays part of the fruit of last night's toil, a watch filched from a pocket unattended in the heat of love. The butter for Moll's breakfast came wrapped in a "Pastoral Letter," an exhortation to virtue by the Bishop of London. At the door, again the future comes. The morals police of the city have found Moll, and in plate four she is beating hemp in Bridewell Prison. The hard life of the prisoners is well documented with whipping post and pillory, and the reforming effects of the reformatory are seen in the look of the woman adjusting her stocking and in the prisoner who, under the nose of the warder, steals Moll's purse.

Lovely woman having stooped to folly, said Hogarth's contemporary, Goldsmith, her only recourse is to die. Hogarth amends the thought. When lovely woman stoops to folly, eventually she contracts a veneral disease (the French disease, it was called in England) and that can be fatal. In plate five, it is. Moll dies as two doctors, centuries before penicillin, argue the merits of their respective cures. Moll's child, unattended, tries to roast a bit of meat on the flame. Moll's nurse rifles her wardrobe. The brief and inevitable harlot's biography is over, but the "progress" isn't and neither is Hogarth. The last plate, *Moll's Funeral*, is not superfluous. Moll is dead but the comedy continues. Far from halting the progress, the funeral becomes an occasion. Moll's coffin becomes a serving bar. Her boy leans against it and winds a top.

58.

WILLIAM HOGARTH,
The Harlot's Progress (plate 1):
The Innocent Country Girl.
Engraving, 1733-34.

59.

WILLIAM HOGARTH,
The Harlot's Progress (plate 2):
She Quarrels with Her Protector.
Engraving.

All over the humble room Moll's trade goes on and the very clergyman called to bless her journey sits with assumed piety: one hand unsteadily holds its gin, the other, under cover of the round clerical hat, makes a progress of its own among the skirts of his neighbor.

This is the quality – toughmindedness – that distinguishes all Hogarth's best prints. Crime may not pay but criminals do not for that reason repent. It is not the immorality but the folly of the progress that fascinates the artist and hardens his vision.

The young artist made a pot of money on Moll's adventures, but he realized at once that he should have made more. Moll became the heroine of poems and plays and china figurines. She also became the heroine of at least eight rapidly produced series of engravings called *The Harlot's Progress*. Historians of the arts can calmly regard all this hurry-up production in London of 1732 as yet another link between prints and movies, the beginning of the cycle theory of stories, but the artist had no such calm. Irritable by nature, Hogarth was outraged by Moll's progress in the hands of his competitors. He had plans for following up his triumph himself, but he refused to feed any more of his ideas to the print pirates of London. The artist turned lobbyist.

Enlisting the aid of fellow artists and various Parliamentary connections, Hogarth embarked on a campaign, which he financed himself, for a copyright law. He proceeded with the paintings for his next series and, from the paintings, did the engravings, but nothing appeared for public sale. In 1735 the act was passed vesting all rights in an artist's productions in the artist himself for a period of fourteen years. The day after the law went into effect Hogarth was on the street with a new series, *The Rake's Progress*. As the title implies, the new series was meant as a companion to the first. In recognition of his success, Hogarth raised the number of prints from six to eight and the price from one guinea to two for the set.

The show begins as Tom Rakewell comes into his inheritance. His deceased father's spirit still lingers in the house and it is against that miserly spirit that Tom's progress takes place. In the portrait over the mantel, the old man is counting his gold. The servant on the ladder spills down coins concealed behind the molding. Mortgages and bonds are piled up at Tom's feet and in a cupboard may be seen a spit, designed for roasting beef but rusting away from long disuse. The attorney seated at the table is the first of the long series of sharpers by whom rake Tom will be swindled.

At the door weeps a ruined girl, sustained by her mother. Hogarth makes a nice thing of hands here. The pregnant girl holds in her hand the ring with which she supposed Tom would wed her. Tom, in his hand, holds the coins to buy her off; the outraged mother swings her fist between the two. Tom's other hand is part of

160.

WILLIAM HOGARTH,
The Harlot's Progress (plate 3):
Apprehended by a Magistrate.
Engraving.

161.

WILLIAM HOGARTH,
The Harlot's Progress (plate 4):
In Bridewell Prison.
Engraving.

another trio of hands, much tighter than the heart-balm trio to the right. Tom's hand holds back his coat as he is measured by a tailor for a suit of mourning. The tailor's hand almost touches Tom's and is balanced by the attorney's, dipping into a sack of coins while Tom is distracted.

Like Moll's, Tom's initial progress is rapid. By plate two the naïve and, on the whole, sympathetic simpleton in luck has taken on all the court of a rich young man about town. On rising he holds levee with his parasites, who, together, constitute a Hogarthian target much more to the point than Tom's poor life. These confidence men are out to fleece the rake of what they can. Hogarth is offering a conducted tour not so much along the road to ruin as through one district of Vanity Fair. Jockey, fencing master, musicians, vie with each other for the favor of the fop. Hogarth's old enemies, the dealers in black paintings, have already taken their percentage of Tom. Between the two portraits of fighting cocks hangs a *Judgment of Paris*. Here, as usually with pictures he uses in his backgrounds, Hogarth makes a double point. The subject relates to the main scene, with Tom as Paris and all these purveyors of fashionable knowledge as the goddesses; and the painting itself types Tom as he types it. Hogarth never hits once if he can hit twice.

The guided tour of hell in the city of London reaches its high point in plate three, *Supper at the Rose*. Sluts and slatterns gather round, spew wine across the table and, in the background, set fire to the world beside a broken mirror. A souvenir of an earlier part of the evening, the lantern stolen from the watchman, lies on the floor. Tom is far gone and his Moll of the moment, in the midst of amorous sport, pinches his watch and passes it on. Across from Tom in the foreground sits and strips the pièce de résistance – or of acquiescence – of the evening. The lady has doffed her corsets and is removing her stockings. Her art, according to reports from that depraved and distant time, is to pose in the nude upon the table with the platter and candle now being brought in. Her utter coolness is one of the chief motives of the print. It is repeated in the girl with Tom's watch and in others and everywhere contrasts with the drunken stupor of Tom. If Hogarth, as he himself often claimed, was a moralist, the moral here is, to the sober belong the spoils.

Everthing after the evening at the Rose Tavern is downhill. On the way to St. James Palace, Tom is arrested for debt. At this point, to our utter astonishment, the ruined girl from plate one is reintroduced, as a result of Hogarth's foolishly listening to moralistic criticism of the *Harlot*. The word was that Moll's descent was too unrelieved by a spark of goodness. Hogarth, obviously knowing in his bones that goodness was no concern of his art, nevertheless tried to get some into the tale of the Rake. Sarah, the

162.

WILLIAM HOGARTH,
The Harlot's Progress (plate 5):
Expires while Doctors Dispute.
Engraving.

163.

WILLIAM HOGARTH,
The Harlot's Progress (plate 6):
The Funeral.
Engraving.

milliner, got pregnant and abandoned by Tom, is goodness, and a very bad thing.

In the seizure for debt scene, Sarah comes forward with her pitiful savings and keeps Tom out of jail. To show his gratitude the Rake marries a rich old horror and has Sarah, her infant and her mother kept out of the church. In the marriage scene, the old fright beams like a girl, Tom surveys the waiting maid, the clergymen are of the general type we already know from the *Harlot*, and, in a corner, two dogs make romantic overtures.

Tom next loses his wedded fortune at a gambling house and is thrown into prison where he is followed by Sarah and his child and by his wife. He is unable even to pay for the beer brought him by a boy. Caught by rival claims upon a love he has only for pleasure, the Rake goes mad, and the last scene presents *Tom in Bedlam*.

It was a fashionable thing in London to drive out to Bedlam of a Sunday afternoon and see the lunatics. For the benefit of those unable to make the journey, Hogarth, following Tom, has opened the doors of the madhouse and, perhaps, suggests the question of relative sanity. Tom, lying naked on the floor in chains, scratches his head in vain; no helpful thought is scratched up. Are his present companions more unhinged than his former? – than the visitors who walk discreetly and peer through a fan at a man who thinks himself king? Beside the king, there's a pope, a musician, a man mad for love, a saint, an astronomer, a map-maker. Are the madmen mad because they think themselves these others, or because they have chosen them for models. And what of Sarah? There Hogarth has had his revenge, for surely the girl, still faithful to her betrayer, is the maddest creature in Bedlam.

All his life Hogarth wanted things from art that he never got. He wanted to be a great artist, to paint historical paintings and frescoes, to have his greatness admitted by his peers. Nobody in eighteenth-century English art ever admitted Hogarth was even in the same line of work as, say, Sir Joshua Reynolds, first president of the Royal Academy and master of the portrait that really looks like the sitter and yet is noble, beautiful, dignified, generous, what you will. Hogarth, of course, wasn't in the same line of work as Sir Joshua, but at the time the feeling was that Sir Joshua's was the one that counted. Hogarth fought that view of art and, at the same time, did his best to meet the high-class standard. For his third great print series he did two things. He had engraved the *Progresses* himself. For *Marriage à la Mode*, he announced in his prospectus, he engaged the services of no less than three accomplished French engravers. They each did two of the six plates and Hogarth did the heads himself. As usual he painted six paintings as models for the engravings.

164.

WILLIAM HOGARTH,
The Rake's Progress (plate 1):
The Young Heir Taking Possession.
Engraving, 1735.

165.

WILLIAM HOGARTH,
The Rake's Progress (plate 3):
The Brothel.
Engraving.

166.

WILLIAM HOGARTH,
The Rake's Progress (plate 4):
The Arrest.
Engraving.

167.

WILLIAM HOGARTH,
The Rake's Progress (plate 8):
The Madhouse.

168.

WILLIAM HOGARTH,
Marriage à la mode (plate 1):
The Contract.
Engraving, 1745.

169.

WILLIAM HOGARTH,
Marriage à la Mode (plate 2):
Breakfast.
Engraving.

The subject itself was a vain attempt at compromise. Hogarth had heard objections to the *Progresses* on many grounds, among them that there was entirely too much low life. He advertised that the new series would be strictly high life, fit to adorn any home, and set about the work.

High life never had a chance.

The theme is the "progress" of a marriage – common enough in the high life of Hogarth's London – contracted for mutual advantage rather than for mutual love. An impoverished earl marries his son to the daughter of a wealthy, ignoble and ambitious businessman. The husband and wife come together, move apart, and come together in mutual catastrophe.

Two scenes create their togetherness. *The Contract* arranges the match. The two fathers exchange credentials, the merchant and his lawyer offering gold, bonds, mortgages, and the assurance of solidity in the plain clothes and attention to detail; the earl's side of the bargain is represented by the aristocratic ailment of gout, by the gold lace on his clothing, his elegant air, his family tree springing from William the Conqueror, and the distant view of the family hall, planned on a fashionable scale and discontinued for lack of funds. The room is hung lavishly with the foreign pictures Hogarth hated. The happy couple themselves ignore the business end of their marriage and the personal as well. The young viscount, sold by his father for solvency, takes a pinch of snuff and gazes at his own true love, his image in a mirror. The merchant's daughter, sold for a title, toys with her ring and listens to Counsellor Silvertongue, a lawyer with a suit of his own to plead. In the corner of the picture two dogs repeat the attitudes of the newly affianced.

Hogarth's own progress was considerable in the ten years between the *Rake* and the *Marriage*. His mastery is nowhere more evident than in plate two, *Breakfast*. Night's candles are burnt out; it is noon, in fact. Viscount Squanderfield, just returned from a night out, sprawls, exhausted, in one chair; his lady stretches luxuriously in the other. The steward, bills and business in hand, turns hopelessly away. A footman in the adjoining room straightens a chair from milady's festivities; another chair, with fiddle and music, is still overturned in the foreground. The plane of the couple continues into the adjoining room, not only to allow Hogarth to take another swipe at the Italian pictures, but to imply the larger world they both inhabit. From the young nobleman's pocket hangs a bit of feminine finery; the lapdog worries it. The contrast between man and wife is subtle and superbly created. Both are tired after a hard night, but his tiredness is that of generations, hers the pleasurable exhaustion of hereditary frugality come at last into its own and loving it.

170.

WILLIAM HOGARTH,
Marriage à la Mode (plate 3):
A Visit to the Quack.
Engraving.

171.

WILLIAM HOGARTH,
Marriage à la Mode (plate 4):
The Levee.
Engraving.

This difference is expressed even in their feet, and the upturned toes are distantly repeated in one of the hated Italian pictures in the next room. A lady's naked foot may be seen, but the rest of her body and what is being done with it are concealed behind a curtain, indicating not so much modesty as discretion: some joys are private. To the private and separate joys of the couple we turn in the next two plates. *A Visit to the Quack*, in Hogarth's time compression, shows not only Squanderfield's private joy, but the pass it has brought him to and a fair guess that no cure will come from the quack. The exhaustion of the viscount at breakfast is now seen as pretty thorough; jaded with the innocent entertainments of Tom Rakewell, the viscount has acquired an eighteenth-century Lolita and with her a case of love's sickness. The girl's vacant face above the gaudy trappings of full-grown harlotry betrays her permanent shock from early introduction to aristocratic pleasure. Her shock concerns no one else in the scene. The viscount is there to complain both about the wight that failed despite the procuress's assurances of the girl's previous virtue, and about the quack's nostrum that hasn't worked. In a closet, a little scene like a medical conference is carried on by a skeleton, a corpse, and the doctor's wig dummy. Viscount, quack, and madam are in lively interchange, bordered by the mask of death on the doctor's table and the mask of horror on the ruined child's face.

Beautifully contrasted to the rather stark and somber quality of the scene with the quack is the next, the *Levee* of the viscountess. Her father-in-law has died and so she has the title she was married for; the coronet over the mirror tells us that, and hanging on the back of her chair is a coral plaything for a child she has borne. Her elegant friends dote on the Italian singer while she and Counsellor Silvertongue arrange for a meeting. The viscount, heir to generationed idleness, requires the stimulation of Lolita; to the city man's robust daughter, plain old-fashioned adultery is still good enough. Hogarth, as always, seizes the chance of striking out at Italian art. Above the lady's head hangs Correggio's orgasmic picture of Io seduced by Jupiter disguised as a cloud. Beginning with the cloud of eloquence released by Silvertongue, the characters of lackeys and toadies form a wonderfully turning line across the scene.

In plate five, Silvertongue succeeds. The viscountess has gone off with him to the London equivalent of Atlantic City for a night of love. In the midst of their celebrations, the viscount enters. The men fight. The counsellor fatally wounds the nobleman and, as the night watchman breaks in at the door, Silvertongue flies out the window, his bare shanks gleaming in the candlelight. The composition, simple and direct, underscores the rapid action. The arc from door to window has its peak with the falling viscount and his chagrined wife; at just that point the arc is crossed by the

172.

WILLIAM HOGARTH,
Marriage à la Mode (plate 5):
Wounded Nobleman.
Engraving.

173.

WILLIAM HOGARTH,
Tail Piece or The Bathos.
Engraving, 1764.

shaft of light from the fireplace we do not see. In that light is the shadow of an andiron, crossed by Silvertongue's blade. The strength of this stark geometry is not diluted by the scattered clothing of the lady and her lover.

Once more, when lovely woman stoops to folly, she finds too late that fate betrays. The viscount is dead, killed by Silvertongue. Silvertongue himself is dead, swung on the gallows, as the paper on the floor informs us. It is his "dying speech," a popular form of imaginative literature in Hogarth's London. There's nothing for it but the countess, too, must die, and die she does, of laudanum, self-administered. Through the window is a glimpse of London Bridge. The masquerade is over and she has come home to die. Her child, a girl, not only ends the Squanderfield line but inherits the weakness of the line. Wearing a leg brace, she is held up to kiss her dying mother. Meanwhile a self-righteous apothecary upbraids the servant for having brought the deadly drug. Meanwhile, too, on one side a starveling cur takes the opportunity to mount the table and eat the roast; on the other, the prudent merchant slips the ring from off his daughter's finger, bringing the whole drama back to where it started. Hogarth, tough-minded to the end, presumes both that the honest businessman will properly have a care for the costly bauble and that the example of the Squanderfields will prevent no one from doing likewise.

All his life Hogarth longed for the fame attendant on "history painting," the noblest of the plastic arts according to the beliefs of his time. He never attained it. Time and again he tried and every time his efforts were coldly received by the judges of these things. These efforts took time and energy away from the field in which he was supremely gifted and more time was drained away, in his last years, by a fruitless political controversy. Looming above the forgotten controversies, a curious book on aesthetics and his diligent efforts to paint in a serious and high-class manner, are Hogarth's immortal views of London life in such prints as *Beer Street* and *Morning* from the *Times of Day*.

In his last year, 1764, Hogarth designed and printed his farewell to the Vanity Fair of the world. *Tailpiece* was designed as the close of a catalogue of his works, and that it is. Old Time himself, so often the unseen mover of Hogarth's pictorial dramas, lies stretched before us, expiring and surrounded by the broken symbols of his reign. On the distant sea a broken vessel sinks beneath the waves. In the sky the sun god dies on his chariot pulled by dying steeds. Toppling over in the foreground is a tavern signboard for "The World's End." Straight down a center perspective the eye is led from that toppling sign to its echo in two dead trees and at last to a distant gallows. It is the end of Hogarth's world but the artist began to draw that end from the first honest look he turned on that world.

174.
WILLIAM HOGARTH,
Beer Street.
Engraving, 1751.

BEER STREET.

Beer, happy Produce of our Isle
Can sinewy Strength impart,
And wearied with Fatigue and Toil
Can chear each manly Heart.

Labour and Art upheld by Thee
Successfully advance,
We quaff Thy' balmy Juice with Glee
And Water leave to France.

Genius of Health, thy grateful Taste
Rivals the Cup of Jove,
And warms each English generous Breast
With Liberty and Love.

Design'd by W. Hogarth.   Publish'd according to Act of Parliament Feb. 1. 1751.   Price 1.

Everything that Hogarth longed for came to Goya, although, t
be sure, it came slowly, laboriously, reluctantly. As the eighteent
century entered its last five years and as Goya turned fifty, he ha
behind him a long and steadily growing accumulation of recogn
tion and reward. Goya came up the hard way, rather like a
officer in a peacetime army, a manager in a totally organized co
poration, or an imperial potentate ascending the "Chairs" of a
American lodge. In some ways eighteenth-century Spain resemble
all three of those institutions.

As a youth Goya tried assiduously to get a place on the bottor
step of the slow-motion escalator. He succeeded, after severa
failures, in getting a major commission. Like a junior executive o
a second lieutenant, he improved his position by marrying int
the establishment; his wife was the sister of the court painte
who was the special favorite of Mengs, the art dictator of Spair
The following year Goya received his first commission for tapestr
cartoons for the royal factory, a profitable business he followe
for sixteen years. Shortly thereafter he began to make etchings c
the masterpieces of Spanish painting in the royal collections.

Connection followed connection. He did church commissions an
painted a long series of court portraits. He was appointed assistan
director of painting at the Academy of San Fernando, Madrid
with the death of his brother-in-law, Goya succeeded him as d
rector. Before that he was made a court painter and presently, a
the post became vacant, Goya was appointed First Court Painter
He had tenure and an assured income even if he never worke
again, a possibility that occurred to him occasionally. He even had
according to various novelistic and cinematic authorities, a ric
and aristocratic mistress who greatly resembled Miss Ava Gard
ner.

On all this Goya turned his back and for some years pursued
largely secret life in art, a life in which he questioned the ver
foundations of the society which had treated him so well and h
expressed himself as far from satisfied with the answers. Th
questions, the answers, and Goya's extremely complex respons
to the answers may be found in three great series of etchings, *Th
Capriccios*, *The Disasters of the War*, and *The Disparates*, o
"follies."

Many explanations have been put forth to explain such a radica
change. Marxists have a fairly easy time demonstrating that th
three series of prints are broadly pro-people and anti-rulers and ar
therefore proto-Marxist. Medical men and materialists generall
can trace this whole new and finally dominant strain in Goya's ar
to a serious illness the painter suffered in 1792, which left him
for the rest of his life, stone deaf. After that people – includin
the Duchess of Alba, the proto-Miss Gardner – communicate
with Goya in writing or by signs; furthermore, Goya's deafnes

175.
FRANCISCO GOYA, 1746-1828
Los Caprichos (plate 1):
Self-portrait.
Etching and aquatint, 1799.

Fran.^{co} Goya y Lucientes,
Pintor.

P. 2

El si pronuncian y la mano alargan
Al primero que llega.

13.

Estan calientes.

176.

FRANCISCO GOYA,
Los Caprichos (plate 2):
They swear to be faithful,
yet marry the first who proposes.

177.

FRANCISCO GOYA,
Los Caprichos (plate 13):
It's hot.

178.

FRANCISCO GOYA,
Los Caprichos (plate 10):
Love and death.

10.

El amor y la muerte.

179.

FRANCISCO GOYA,
Los Caprichos (plate 15):
Good advice.

180.

FRANCISCO GOYA,
Los Caprichos (plate 14):
What a sacrifice!

181.

FRANCISCO GOYA,
Los Caprichos (plate 33):
To the Count Palatine.

Bellos consejos.

Que sacrificio!

Al Conde Palatino.

was filled with buzzing noises of the kind suggested by many of the more fantastic *Capriccios*. Again, what we may call the Gardnerites have been arguing for years – long before Miss Gardner's birth – that a love affair with the Duchess of Alba was chiefly responsible for the despair, melancholy and all-around depression so evident in the prints. Finally, psychiatrists find in the prints all they need to dissect the printmaker. There is a great deal of flying, both by birds and by humans; there are even lessons in flying; there is fascination with death and torture hardly to be explained by the fact that Spain was filled with death and torture; there are metamorphoses from human to animal and the reverse; there are curious juxtapositions of young ladies and horses. There are even, rather disappointingly, prints that overtly refer to courtship, marriage and sex. Clearly Goya, like everybody else from Sophocles to Dostoevski, was a proto-Freudian.

On the other hand, one is free to believe that the more interesting and profitable question is not, What does psychiatry think of Goya, but rather, What would Goya think of psychiatry?

It might even be possible to sketch an answer. Such a sketch would begin with the fact that, like most Spanish intellectuals of his time and since, Goya was anticlerical. Anticlericalism is not an attitude toward religion; it does not mean that one leaves off believing that God made the world and begins believing that Sir Julian Huxley made it. Anticlericalism is not philosophic thought, but social thought; as the name implies, it only exists in the presence of and in opposition to clericalism. Clericalism is both a state of mind and a social organization produced by that state of mind. It begins with the proposition that God is the supreme good, a proposition that proves itself in the defining of the terms. Clericalism then proceeds to organize every aspect of society toward that supreme good and it turns out in every case that what is good for clerics, the people administering the Church, is necessarily good for God. Among several other characteristics, the social structure of Goya's Spain was definitely clerical. Among many other characteristics, his prints are consistently anticlerical. The only force in twentieth-century America that remotely approaches Spanish clericalism is psychiatry in its wider, extraclinical manifestations in fields as far as sociology and sales techniques.

Actually there is a standard literary phenomenon in America that parallels very closely Goya's sudden revelation of subversive depths beneath the official activities of the king's artist. This is the editorial employee of Time, Inc., who, like Goya, reaches the age of fifty and makes his move. The move consists, usually, of writing a book to show that *Time*'s publisher, Mr. Henry Luce, strongly favors the Republican Party, a character flaw, it should be noted, that Mr. Luce shares with most of his fellow news publishers. This established feature of the literary scene is accept-

82.
FRANCISCO GOYA,
Los Caprichos (plate 36):
A bad night.

83.
FRANCISCO GOYA,
Los Caprichos (plate 41):
No more, no less.

Mala noche.

Ni mas ni menos.

ed without recourse to Marxism, medicine, romance, or psychiatry, and Goya's prints can be so accepted too. The Spaniard devoted half a lifetime to becoming Court Painter and then discovered that he was a court painter. The difference between the exposé of Mr. Luce's GOPartisanship and Goya's prints is one of quality and comes from the fact that Goya was a genius.

Almost any given print in the *Capriccios* is an extraordinary thing. Together the eighty prints are a brilliant, cynical, witty commentary on life in Spain at the end of the eighteenth century and on life in highly organized society any time, any place.

The series opens with that cool portrait of the artist as a skeptical observer. This is followed by an extended exposition of the varieties of love and marriage, the basic social contract, broken here and there by scenes of private vices: a miser clutching his gold, greedy monks burning their lips, a drunkard setting his house on fire. The love and marriage pictures equate the official marriage à-la-mode with the vigorous sex life of the Madrid streets conducted by the *majos* and *majas* of the working class.

In part the subject matter is the same as Hogarth's, but the differences are profound. Hogarth's scenes of London low life and high life take place on a kind of box stage, a theatrical set which perfectly reproduces the details of London interiors and exteriors. In Goya's scenes, there is also a stage suggestion, but the set is absent. The characters themselves are spotlighted against a backdrop composed of the luminous, shadowy, ambiguous lights of aquatint, the new etching process that Goya made completely his own. The pebbled grain of the aquatint ranges from rich black to very lightly sketched grays, approximating the wash in wash drawings. Throughout the prints, Goya thoroughly exploits the possible range of the medium, but in any single print he is more apt to limit the range to two or three tones. Against this glowing and darkling background, the characters move from the comedy of Madrid into the comedy of life.

After the self-portrait, the series proper opens with a marriage of indifference, titled by Goya, "They swear to be faithful, yet marry the first who proposes." The blindfolded bride goes to the altar against the bored regard of the crowd. Three scenes of fashionable flirtation are succeeded by three consequences: a rape, a dead mistress, and a lover dead in a duel. Marriage à la mode is repeated to Goya's comment, "What a sacrifice!" Then, almost imperceptibly, fashionable marriage is modulated into prostitution as a social institution, with an apprentice receiving "good counsel" from an old pro and the "plucking" of the victims going on apace. A plucker is plucked herself by the noble attorneys who manage the enterprise. Prostitutes are punished by the Holy Inquisition and it is difficult to choose between the condemned girl and her inquisitors. The quack doctor, "Count Palatine," applies his vio-

Tu que no puedes.

Mucho hay que chupar.

184.

FRANCISCO GOYA,
Los Caprichos (plate 42):
They cannot help it.

185.

FRANCISCO GOYA,
Los Caprichos (plate 45):
There's a lot to suck.

186.

FRANCISCO GOYA,
Los Caprichos (plate 43):
The dream of reason produces monsters.

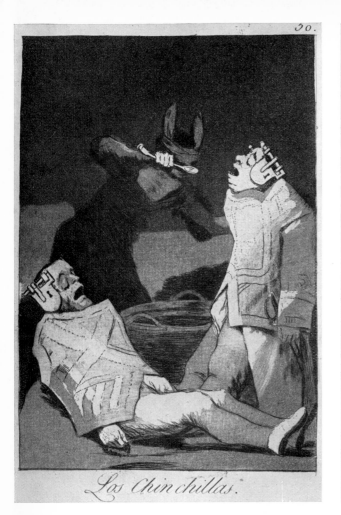

Los Chinchillas.

Se repulen

187.

FRANCISCO GOYA,
Los Caprichos (plate 50):
The Chinchilla rats.

188.

FRANCISCO GOYA,
Los Caprichos (plate 51):
They pare their own nails.

189.

FRANCISCO GOYA,
Los Caprichos (plate 57):
The betrothal.

La filiacion

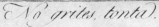
No grites, tonta.

Quien lo creyera!

190.

FRANCISCO GOYA,
Los Caprichos (plate 74):
Don't cry, idiot.

191.

FRANCISCO GOYA,
Los Caprichos (plate 62):
Who would believe it?

192.

FRANCISCO GOYA,
Los Caprichos (plate 63):
Look, are we not wonderful!

Miren que grabes!

lent ministrations to victims of the trade. A Madrid Delilah wields the razor on her feminized and melting victim, and the first half closes with the tribulations of a streetwalker on a "bad night."

Between the first and second "acts" of Goya's comedy occurs an interlude of six plates recognized by his fellow Madrileños as a brief essay on Manuel Godoy, the queen's lover who, because of satisfaction rendered in that capacity, moved rapidly, while still in his early twenties, from guardsman to foreign minister to grandee of Spain to prime minister and ruler of the country. Godoy, by his high degree of corruption and incompetence, was an outstanding candidate for the title of Spain's evil genius during a period full of such candidates, all well qualified.

Godoy appears as an ass, the same way he appeared to Madrileños of all parties. His genealogy and heraldry are prepared for the ass, as they were for Godoy. The ass has his portrait painted by a talented ape. The ass as doctor takes the pulse of the patient – Spain: the Monarchy? – and is asked by Goya, "Of which sickness will he die?" The interlude ends as two asses seat themselves comfortably on the backs of two citizens: there is more to government by asses than Manuel Godoy.

The second act opens with one of the great enduring images that printmaking has given the world. Again, a self-portrait; but now the artist sleeps, arms and head on his desk among the tools of his trade. As he sleeps the grainy background comes alive with winged creatures: giant bats and owls of the night. On the floor crouches a cat, alert and enormous. On the side of the artist's desk appear the words, in white on gray: *El sueño de la razón produce monstruos*, "The dream of reason produces monsters."

That theme is the story of modern times. From Goya's day to ours, monsters have come forth supported by and even engendered by some dream of reason. The dream of Marx produced Stalin. The dream of a "New Order" in Europe produced – in that sweetly reasonable phrase – "the final solution of the Jewish problem" at Auschwitz and Belsen. The dream of gentle Einstein produced the light at Hiroshima. Goya, living at the end of the Age of Reason and the beginning of the age of monsters, saw and recorded the classic instance of what happens when dreams come true: when the dream of liberty, equality, and fraternity produced first the Terror, then Napoleon.

Monsters inhabit the whole second half of the *Capriccios*. Immediately after the sleeping self-portrait, mysterious crones appear, engaged in collecting infants. The crones continue and are joined by a race of dwarfs, frequently got up as monks. Educational efforts are made as an owl lectures to monks and "chinchillas" – little rats – eyes closed, straitjacketed and ears padlocked, are spoonfed by the ass-man, himself wearing a blindfold.

The monsters are interested in personal appearance. "They pare

195.
FRANCISCO GOYA,
Disparates (plate 3):
Strange folly.

196.
FRANCISCO GOYA,
Disparates (plate 8):
People in sacks.

197.

FRANCISCO GOYA,
Disparates (plate 10):
*Young woman
on a bucking horse.*

198.

FRANCISCO GOYA,
Disparates (plate 13):
One way to fly.

their own nails," Goya notes. Thus well-groomed they present themselves to young ladies who are not nearly as reluctant as they seem. "You can't escape," Goya cautions, and "Don't cry, idiot," to a maiden who can barely conceal her joy at being attacked.

Human activity is no less intense. *The Betrothal* records a marriage between ancestors while the bride hides any identity she may have. This leads to husband and wife roped together, surmounted by one of the monsters and asking, "Will no one set us free?" Such human associations deliver humanity to the monsters – of whatever kind – and a battling couple drifts into the abyss and into waiting claws and fangs.

Humanity and the monsters come together in witchcraft, itself both the dream of reason and the sleep of reason. Witchcraft, by any description, is primarily an effort to find a short cut to knowledge and power. Votaries take the oath of obedience and struggle to master the typical witchly activity of flying. In all these efforts, the would-be witches are not figures of terror but figures of depraved human ambition. Again and again the effort is made and finally the witches do get off the ground. But already the witching hour is drawing to a close. "Day breaks, we must away," says a bony hag to her companions. Returning to daylight, we note an incompetent official and end with a group of stupid monks. They do the housework; they drink in the cellar. They yawn themselves to sleep. "It is the hour," closes the *Capriccios*. Like most of Goya's prints, the scene and the line have more than one meaning; it's a safe bet that Goya meant them all.

The *Capriccios* were published in 1799, and withdrawn from public sale almost immediately. Twenty-seven sets were sold. With the Holy Inquisition looking into the matter and preparing material for a trial, Goya, in 1803, presented the copper plates and the remaining two hundred and forty printed sets to the king, thus giving his work a measure of royal protection and obtaining a pension for his son. In 1806 the Spanish government issued a new edition – with Godoy's permission – and Spanish governments ever since have been running off new impressions from the plates. Goya did not make the same mistake again. *The Disasters of the War* was etched between 1808 and 1820, the *Disparates* during the latter part of the same period. Neither set was published by Goya. He left them behind as a memorandum to posterity. Appropriately, they appeared during the American Civil War.

The *Disparates*, in twenty-two plates, are, in a sense, the completion of the *Capriccios*. The subjects are the same and the presentations have the same air of tantalizing enigma, but there are great differences. In the twenty years or so between the two sets, Goya doubtless perfected his mastery of etching and aquatint, as is evidenced by the *Tauromaquia* (*The Art of Bullfighting*),

.

NCISCO GOYA,
parates (plate 22):
olish extravagance.
b. 1877.

LLUVIA DE TOROS
(Pluie de Taureaux)

etched and published in the interim. That he also deepened h way of looking at things may be learned from the *Disasters* a from his part in the events they portray. The new depth is al evident in the *Disparates.* There frequently is a tone of capri appropriate to the title in the earlier set. The sex adventurers the first part and the witches of the second all appear with certain liveliness. They are all engaged in the dance of life; a the music, sometimes even lilting music, is implied in the li and in the disposition of the figures in the space of the pictur None of this is present in the *Disparates.* For one thing, there a no little sequences of pictures to establish that kind of rhyth Each *Disparate* appears unrelated to the others except as all gether establish a somber, deliberated view of what man is.

The music of the *Disparates* is the music of utter silence. T silence perhaps is imposed by the aquatint. Light or dark, it no longer background. Its grain is the texture of the univer and the figures appear not against it but out of it, as if emergi from fog or fashioned out of the primal stuff of creation. T figures seem larger, too, than those of the *Capriccios*, fixed f ever in their attitudes, fixed forever in their silence.

The series begins like the *Capriccios* with *Feminine Folly*; s women, all with an air of innocent detachment, hold a blank full of diminutive males and toss them in the air as if they we stuffed puppets. Next, the *Folly of Fear* terrifies an army with figure no more substantial than the puppets, made of yardgoo draped on scaffolding. A large family appears out on the limb a tree; there is only the limb, all else is lost in the grainy m and the family seems quite at home.

The efforts of the witches in the *Capriccios* is recalled in *Flig of Folly* and again in *A Mode of Flight.* In both, aerodynami have been solved, but the calm figures, unlike the witches, not really fly: they hover. The people who are *Sacked* mainta aristocratic dignity and give no hint they are aware of their co dition. A rearing stallions turns and bites the dress of the wom he has thrown; she flings her arms wide and assumes the sm of ecstasy. The *Matrimonial Folly* that formerly tied two disp rate people together has now let them grow into each other permanently disfigured living corpses, surrounded by the praye and laughter of society. The aquatint grows darker. Out of it, the very end, emerge the mysterious, heroic, tragic symbols Spain, the bulls of combat and slaughter.

The historical background of *The Disasters of the War* is co plicated and not really necessary to an appreciation of the eigh three plates. The cumulating impact of the scenes of death a despair addresses itself to one of the basic human experiences, t of having one's country occupied and ravaged by hostile armi Since Goya etched the plates, the experience has been shared

Tristes presentimientos de lo que ha de acontecer.

)0.

ʀᴀɴᴄɪsᴄᴏ ɢᴏʏᴀ,
ᴐs *Desastres de la Guerra*
late 1):
Ioomy presentiments
things to come.
tching and aquatint, 1808-1820, pub. 1863.

Con razon ó sin ella.

201.

FRANCISCO GOYA,
Los Desastres de la Guerra
(plate 2):
With reason or without.

202.

FRANCISCO GOYA,
Los Desastres de la Guerra
(plate 7):
What courage!

Que valor!

203.

FRANCISCO GOYA,
Los Desastres de la Guerra
(plate 13):
Bitter presence.

204.

FRANCISCO GOYA,
Los Desastres de la Guerra
(plate 15):
And there is no remedy.

Amarga presencia.

Y no hai remedio.

205.

FRANCISCO GOYA,
Los Desastres de la Guerra
(plate 32):
Why?

206.

FRANCISCO GOYA,
Los Desastres de la Guerra
(plate 47):
Thus it happened.

Por qué?

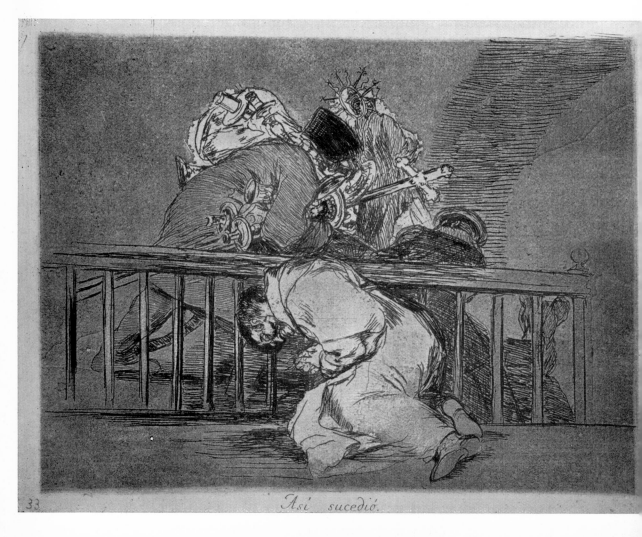

Así sucedió.

207.

FRANCISCO GOYA,
Los Desastres de la Guerra (plate 48):
Cruel suffering!

208.

FRANCISCO GOYA,
Los Desastres de la Guerra (plate 61):
Do they belong to another race?

Cruel lástima!

Si son de otro linage.

least once by every nation of the West except Sweden and the northern part of the United States.

Still, Goya drew of the disaster of *the* war, not of war in general; and the Peninsular Campaign had certain distinctive features that marked it out from the wars of the past and began the pattern of wars since then. The dream of reason of the French Revolution passed very rapidly from the death of kings to the coronation of the emperor and with him a whole new batch of kings as Napoleon set members of his *nouveau puissant* family upon all the thrones of Europe. In 1808 the French invaded and occupied Spain, under pretext of fulfilling treaty obligations. The Bourbon king, Ferdinand VII, was deposed and Joseph Bonaparte named king of Spain. Then two surprising things happened.

Napoleon had already made war a national enterprise by introducing conscription. The Spanish people introduced guerrilla warfare as a popular enterprise and threw themselves into the impossible task of taking on the best organized army since the Romans with little besides their bare hands. The resistance dragged on for six years of cruelty and oppression, and was beaten finally not by the French but by disease and famine.

The second thing was the immediate desertion of the Bourbon cause by the Bourbons. Ferdinand declared himself overjoyed to welcome Joseph Bonaparte and tried to negotiate a marriage alliance between himself and some Bonaparte female. Napoleon popped him into cushioned custody and sent him Parisian actresses to keep his mind off the reign in Spain. The higher clergy, who, along with the higher aristocracy, had joined in their king's submission, sent him a Peruvian Tartuffe as confessor, to keep his mind off the actresses.

The resistance therefore took on democratic coloration, both from a revival of the ancient Spanish tradition of free villages and from the new thought of the Liberals. With the fall of Napoleon and the restoration of Ferdinand, the Bourbon king and the Spanish Church combined to reimpose clerical absolutism. The absolutists, however, were hopelessly inefficient in most government affairs except the prosecution of independent thought and speech. England and Czarist Russia for a while competed for Ferdinand's worthless favor but the final crushing of liberty took place with a second French invasion, this one in 1823 by the troops of the restored French monarchy. Ferdinand and the Inquisition began a continuing persecution of the intellect and of freedom. Goya, at the age of seventy-eight, left the country and settled at Bordeaux, where he died in 1828, active and working almost to the end.

The *Disasters* open with a plate etched after most of the series was complete, *Forebodings of Things to Come*. The scratchy night is alive with dimly seen monsters. On the hard earth kneels

Nada. Ello dirá.

209.

FRANCISCO GOYA,
Los Desastres de la Guerra (plate 69):
Nothing. It speaks for itself.

210.

FRANCISCO GOYA,
Los Desastres de la Guerra (plate 73):
Cat's pantomime.

Gatesca pantomima.

Farándula de charlatanes.

211.

FRANCISCO GOYA,
Los Desastres de la Guerra (plate 75):
The charlatans' swindle.

212.

FRANCISCO GOYA,
Los Desastres de la Guerra (plate 77):
The cord breaks.

Que se rompe la cuerda.

Si resucitará?

213.

FRANCISCO GOYA,
Los Desastres de la Guerra (plate 80):
Will she rise again?

214.

FRANCISCO GOYA,
Los Desastres de la Guerra (plate 79):
Truth is dead.

Murió la Verdad

the patient and fearful figure of the Spanish man of the people, awaiting the worst, knowing it will come. In that single plate Goya wrote the history of his people for over a century ahead.

Then the massacre begins. The French Mamelukes throughout the series are portrayed as rigid, frightful robots going about their business like machines of murder. The Spanish women, sometimes with babes in arms, join their men in resisting the oppressor. In plate seven, Goya presents the single instance of his unqualified admiration: "What valor!" he exclaims at the graceful form of a woman, on a pile of corpses, firing a captured cannon into the murky grain where the enemy awaits.

The French slaughter begins in earnest and begins with a series of attacks on women, culminating in a rape scene in a cellar, with a Spanish male prisoner tied fast to witness the debauching of his woman. The gallows begin their work; and the firing squads, as on the famous night of May 2, 1808, go into action. Corpses begin to pile up. French soldiers, intent on rape, are briefly recalled by their commander to the more pressing tasks of murder: "No more time." Like the relentless beating of the drums of execution, the slaughter goes on. The people rise against the French with a fury no less monstrous, and the French increase the tempo. Bodies of violated women are dumped into cellars. Hanging and mutilation begin. If a tree isn't high enough, the French make up for gravity by tugging the victim against the noose. Heads and hands are cut off and impaled on stumps of trees. The people flee before the monsters from the French dream of reason as from a plague. Across the open, lighted, arid country they run, children and goods on their shoulders. The night comes down as the first great movement of the *Disasters* ends. "This is bad," Goya comments as the Mamelukes impale a priest on a sword, and "Thus it happened," as they carry off the church vessels and images from the altar and the priest sinks at the communion rail.

Goya, the impassioned pictorial journalist, needs no formal interlude like that used by Goya, the sardonic commentator on social caprice. The guerrilla war ends with the French looting of the church. The visual montage cuts abruptly to Madrid and the background. From a group of dead or worn-out citizens two figures arise: a mother sits up holding her child, and a man stands, holding out his hat in the eternal gesture of the beggar: *Cruel suffering!* The camera eye of Goya's imaginative recollection of those days moves slowly and heartbreakingly through the starvation of a city. The aquatint grain appears like bloody hail, frozen and floating in the air and on the earth. A military policeman stands between the starving and the well-fed: *As if they were a different species.* Again, the night comes down and women wander among their dead. The famine sequence ends, as sharply

215.
FRANCISCO GOYA,
The Giant.
Aquatint, c. 1819.

as it began, with the graceful body of a dead woman being handed down for burial by a chain of workers.

In the final, swift movement of the *Disasters*, Napoleon has been overthrown and the country is returning to a normality it has been fighting against ever since. From an official writing at a desk, Spanish women turn away in despair and the dogs bark at them. The images of a sterile and superstitious religion are hauled back into place first by an ass and next on the backs of aristocrats. Spoon in hand, a monk squats among the images and, for a moment, the dead of Spain seem to rise from the earth still in pain; but the word the dead man writes is "Nada." Nothing. The monsters return on obscene wings and a cleric in vestments makes his obeisance before their altar. The indignant camera of Goya's intellect swings around: we see the cleric from the front, on his knees; his own head has become a parrot's and the claws coming out of his robes summon a congregation of asses, wolves, and brutalized Spaniards to worship. A priest walks a tightrope. There is a funeral scene: a bishop presides as other clerics shovel in the dirt; the corpse is a bare-bosomed woman supine, hands crossed. *Truth is dead.* In the following plate, the dying light from Truth's head has blazed up again. Ecclesiastics and officials fall back into the shadows and Goya asks, *If she should rise?*

Rise she did, within a very short time of the etching of that plate. She was, thanks to the trade union of European monarchy, thrust down again and Goya went into exile. What seems to have been his last etched plate was *The Giant*. The plate was large and it cracked after only three impressions were printed. The technique is aquatint handled by a master. The whole plate was given a deep aquatint tone and then figures and highlights were created by burnishing and scraping, a final bit of indirection by a master of that mode. The great figure sits on the edge of the world as the night comes on. The sliver moon is up and most things are in shadow, but the dying sun casts light upon the shoulders and parts of the face of the giant. He looks up, still interested in what may be seen and in what it may mean. Perhaps the plate was Goya's last self-portrait.

Chapter Ten

Daumier

Toward the end of his long life as painter and etcher, Goya, in exile at Bordeaux, made a few prints in the newly invented process of lithography. When Goya died, in 1828, a twenty-year-old Parisian, Honoré Daumier, was perfecting both a mastery of the lithograph and a social point of view admirably suited to the new print form and to the adventures of France during Daumier's lifetime.

The adventures, of course, are still going on, and not only in France. In that country, however, there has always been a certain special quality about the adventures, for it was in France that they began. The French Revolution posed an enormous threat to all authorities in all areas of life in all countries. The "adventures" in politics and economics that Daumier watched so closely and portrayed so brilliantly are generally of two kinds: the direct attempt to erase the Revolution from history and thus restore all things as they were before the deluge; and the judo-like attempt to turn the force of the Revolution to one's own ends and against the ends of liberty, equality, and fraternity. The ideal of the fathers, Péguy noted, was to die for the Republic; the ideal of the sons was to live off it.

The two adventures, and certainly the two different kinds of adventurer, went frequently together. The two were not only allied but embodied in a single person by the time Daumier was adult and aware of the France that was to be his model and his public for almost half a century. The person was Louis-Philippe, the last king of France. Napoleon himself had successfully turned the Revolution into an expression of his military genius and vulgar tastes. When his dream of reason went bankrupt the receivers were the absolutists of Europe. They didn't much care who ruled France so long as it wasn't the French people. The last of a trio of handmade kings was Louis-Philippe. His reign coincided with the rise of a new class, the entrepreneurs, capitalists, and speculators who had made their fortunes in the chaos of the Revolution and were determined, under the revived monarchy, to expand them. Louis-Philippe, the "bourgeois king," identified himself completely with the new class and invited its members to help themselves to the public and private wealth of France. They fell to with a will.

The Revolution, however, had left another creation behind, the popular press. Large parts of the press, then as now, were for sale, but the very availability of papers for purchase by political parties or entrepreneurs at least insures the possibility of some parts of the press remaining free. To that free press the young Daumier attached himself and became the first great artist in lithography.

Senefelder's magical stone had the precise virtues needed for the popular press. Daumier drew directly on the stone, thus elimi-

16.

HONORÉ DAUMIER, 1808-1879,
*Very humble, very submissive,
very obedient and above
all very voracious subjects.*
Lithograph, 1832.

17.

HONORÉ DAUMIER,
*Ring down the curtain,
the farce is over.*
Lithograph, 1834.

 Pl. 421

Baissez le rideau la farce est jouée

nating all the steps between drawn comment and the plate prepared for printing. Speed and directness are essential to the
political and social artist and never more so than in a period of
rapid change. The lithographic stone also permitted large numbers
of impressions, a quality that has more than technical implications.
The lithographic artist was thus in almost daily, always direct
contact with a public limited only by the appeal of the work
itself. In his professional career as graphic journalist and edito-
rialist, Daumier made some four thousand lithographs, many
more drawings, and a respectable number of paintings and pieces
of sculpture, all of them informed by his capacity for social indignation, by expressive line and by his eye for flaws and dangers
to the France he loved.

Daumier was presented with his profession by the man who
invented it, the editor Charles Philipon, whose two papers, the
Charivari and the *Caricature*, began preparing the revolution of
1848 almost as soon as Louis-Philippe became king in 1830.

As early as 1832, Daumier made his own contribution to Philipon's war with the monarchy. *Gargantua*, named for the giant
in Rabelais, shows the king as an endlessly hungry ogre, fed by
assiduous ministers of state and new industrialists; in goes the
gold, out come contracts and patents of nobility for stock jobbers
and swindlers, as the working people are exploited to pay for
the feast. The Gargantuan hunger of the new regime was not
confined to the monarch himself. The throne, occupied only by
the choice prizes of government, dominates a herd of the new
men feeding like swine to Daumier's description of them: *Very
Humble, Very Submissive, Very Obedient and Above All Very
Voracious Subjects.*

Louis-Philippe, the "Pear King" as Daumier and Philipon styled
him, did not take these attacks from a free press without protest.
With Daumier the protest took the form of a fine of five hundred
francs and six months in prison. Daumier thus began the tradition
of the journalist in jail.

He continued the attack on Louis-Philippe and in the process
rose to his first great achievements as journalist-printmaker. The
king's dissolution of the French legislature is recorded with
another line from Rabelais, *Ring Down the Curtain, the Farce
is Over*. Louis-Philippe as the clown Pierrot suspends represent-
ative government. The legislature itself, "very submissive, very
obedient," became the classic model for corrupt lawmakers in
The Legislative Belly. The anatomy of the legislators, large as it
is, is enlarged further in the very architecture of their chamber
seen by Daumier as row upon expanding row, each dedicated to
the fat and flabby in spirit as well as body. The Marquis de
Lafayette, the same soldier who played a part in the American
Revolution, was, as an old man, a focus for opposition to the

LE VENTRE LÉGISLATIF.

Aspect des bancs ministériels de la chambre improstituée de 1834.

218.

HONORÉ DAUMIER,
The legislative belly.
Lithograph, 1834.

219.

HONORÉ DAUMIER,
Lafayette done for.
Lithograph, 1834.

ENFONCÉ LAFAYETTE!... ATTRAPE, MON VIEUX!

bourgeois king and Daumier pictures the hypocritical grief of Louis-Philippe at Lafayette's funeral. Here, as in *Ring Down the Curtain*, the pear-shaped figure of the king passes beyond political satire of the moment and joins the gallery of human types not so much created as perceived and fixed forever by literature and art.

The actual Louis-Philippe, far from being grateful at being thus assured a place in the history of human achievement, began the inevitable encroachment of freedom of the press. Daumier warned him off by pointing to the fate of one of his predecessors, Charles X, in *Don't Meddle with the Press!* Laws against the poor seeking justice and against the press seeking truth became rapidly more severe and more severely enforced. In a police raid in a poor district of Paris, Louis-Philippe's agents murdered the family of an innocent workingman. Daumier commemorated the event in a great lithograph named for the address and the day of the police murders, *Rue Transnonain, April 15, 1834.* The stark shaft of light across the center of the picture combines the confusion of the bedclothes with the bayoneted corpse in his nightshirt. The foreshortening of the body compresses the sense of quiet outrage which is given great impetus from the almost hidden body of the child beneath the body of its father. On the right, the staring eyes of a dead old man emphasize another depth sounded by the regime. On the left, the shadows seem calm and peaceful behind the glare of massacre in the center of the picture. But in those gray grainy shadows we see the humble articles of toilet of the urban poor and on the floor the lifeless body of the woman of the house.

The straightforward realism of the portrayal contrasts sharply with the exaggerated caricature of Daumier's other political lithographs. At this point, the style says, the reign of Louis-Philippe has gone beyond parody. The representation of the facts alone is more powerful and more damaging than any comment by distortion. The event provides its own commentary.

It would be pleasant to record that these powerful blows for freedom had their intended effect. They did not. More than a dozen years later the revolution of 1848 toppled Louis-Philippe from his throne and no doubt the work of Daumier and Philipon was a factor of some kind in the final explosion. But the immediate result of the attack was the passing of the "September Laws" making journalistic opposition illegal. *Caricature* went out of business. Philipon and Daumier directed their attention to other aspects of the brave new world of the bourgeois king. The king had made himself safe. It was the turn of the bourgeois.

There followed, over a period of two years, Daumier's first great lithographic series, the one hundred pictures of the ingenuity, roguery, and energy of Robert Macaire, the very epitome of the

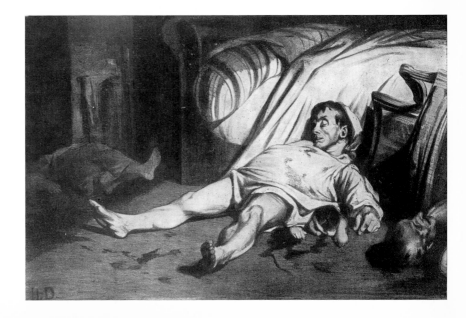

220.

Don't meddle with the press.
Lithograph, 1834.

221.

Rue Transnonain, April 15, 1834.
Lithograph, 1834.

new men. The Macaire adventures do not constitute a consecutive story, as do, for example, the *Progresses* of Hogarth. They show, rather, the arrival in France of the promoter, Robert Macaire, and his explosion into all fields of human activity. The optimistic, fast-talking Macaire spins dreams of fortune to all who listen, and makes his own fortune out of their desire for something for nothing. He is accompanied by the skinny, down-at-the-heels Bertrand, a kind of Sancho Panza to the knight of enterprise. At their first appearance, Macaire, himself almost in rage, announces his love of "industry" and his intention to plunder the Bank of France, financiers, "all the world." Bertrand cautions, "But the police?" To which Macaire replies, in the spirit of the age, "You are an animal, Bertrand. Who would arrest a millionaire?"

That kind of one-paragraph story accompanied each of the lithographs and was written by Philipon. Yet it is no more proper to say that Daumier illustrated the writing of his friend than to say, as is said occasionally, that Daumier illustrated Balzac. Rather, Balzac and Daumier – and Philipon as well – were keenly aware of the new tone in Paris life in the thirties and forties, a tone of strident opportunism backed by ruthless manipulation of public confidence and public institutions.

When pressed by need, Macaire is capable of begging in the streets, but even then he surrounds his act with an aura of fallen grandeur, of a nobleman come on evil days; he is *Robert Macaire, the Distinguished Beggar.* And he is distinguished. He holds his hand with elegance and inflates his rags with a sense of destiny momentarily in pawn. But, even in rags, he is more at home on the platform of a hired carriage, with Bertrand beating the drum as Macaire cries his worthless shares of stock: "Ladies and gentlemen, silver mines, gold mines, diamond mines...." As Robert Macaire pushes his merchandise, the shares do acquire a value beyond their intrinsic value of waste paper. They represent, in the first instance, the dreams of avarice of the customers; more negotiably, they represent a created demand which is nonetheless real for being a demand for that which does not exist.

In a similar way, Robert Macaire himself takes on a certain specious reality as the series progresses. He more than half-believes his own incessant propaganda; he is wholly identified with the preposterous public figure he has created for himself. He moves confidently through swindle after swindle, examining all aspects of Parisian life for the opportunities they present to the man of enterprise. As he makes his examinations and calculates his risks, Robert Macaire improves his dress and so enhances his own reality. The tense line of that leg, the jaunty tilt of the hat, the muffler about the chin and the eager innocence of the face create a type that is with us yet.

Macaire becomes a lawyer, a doctor, a dentist, a druggist, but

222.

HONORÉ DAUMIER,
Robert Macaire, distinguished beggar.
Lithograph, 1837.

223.

HONORÉ DAUMIER,
Ladies and Gentlemen, silver mines...
Lithograph, 1836.

224.

HONORÉ DAUMIER,
Bertrand, I adore industry.
Lithograph, 1836.

always and everywhere an "agent of affairs," in the French phrase that is so much more Macaire than "business agent." The telephone booth being still in the future, the streets of Paris were his office, hearth and home — somebody else's were equally his, as in *Exploitation of Love*. No human sentiment, particularly those shared by most of mankind, is foreign to Macaire's promotion, as in his touching speech at the grave of his mother. Toward the end of the series, looking at the France around him, Macaire could open his heart to Bertrand: "All the same it is flattering to have made so many disciples." Deeply sensitive to the limits of gullibility, Macaire takes his exit with grace, with sacks of money and with a touching farewell to *La Patrie*, while the practical Bertrand hurries him across the frontier. Daumier found other things to do, but Robert Macaire had lived before Daumier and easily survived him. Macaire went to America; when the Securities Exchange Commission caused his retirement from finance, he went into television, where he writes, directs, and plays all the parts in many of the entertainments and all of the commercials.

As for Daumier, he cast his eye upon the rest of Paris. The artist had begun life, when he was fourteen, as a law-court messenger and he brought his early memories up to date in a memorable series on the *Men of Justice*. "You have lost your suit, it is true," the lawyer consoles his client, "but you have had the pleasure of hearing me argue." In the figure of the defeated advocate there is, perhaps, a touch of the Macaire line, as there is in many of the Parisian types Daumier drew.

That line can even become feminine, or at least be used to show a feminine phenomenon, *Les Bas-Bleus* or *The Blue Stockings*, who were then taking over the writing of sentimental literature. Daumier showed the literary ladies moving in on libraries, press clubs and the ancient process of mutual boosting. He noted that the Blue Stockings fared forth to literary business, leaving their husbands at home as nursemaids. Like Macaire, the Blue Stockings crossed the Atlantic, where they went into the magnolia business with steady success.

In Paris, as in America, there was a great vogue for the manners and buildings of ancient Rome and Greece. The bourgeois thought to turn themselves into the gods and heroes of antiquity. Daumier reversed the process. In a series of lithographs called *Ancient History*, he portrayed the immortals and mortals of old in the bodies and faces of his contemporaries in Paris. The love of Hero and Leander, thwarted by the waters of the Hellespont, is aided by water wings. *The Night of Love* at the end of the Odyssey finds Odysseus in bed with Penelope enjoying what he had long missed, a good night's sleep. Throughout the series, the romantic and faraway is turned into the prosaic, comic, and everyday.

225.

HONORÉ DAUMIER,
You have lost your suit, it's true.
Lithograph, 1848.

226.

HONORÉ DAUMIER,
I thought to name my drama.
Lithograph, 1844.

227.

HONORÉ DAUMIER,
Hero and Leander.
Lithograph, 1842.

In 1848 Daumier had the opportunity to pay his last respects to Louis-Philippe, as the bourgeois king departed for bourgeois England and liberty returned to France. The artist noted an arrival to balance the departure, the *Napoleonic Packetboat*. Throughout the brief life of the second republic, France was alive with a new set of enemies of liberty, the followers of Louis Napoleon, determined to revive the empire. To depict their efforts, their characters and their style, Daumier invented a sinister figure, Ratapoil. Propagandist, political dirty worker, Ratapoil bore a distinct resemblance to Louis Napoleon. Wearing the beard and mustaches of the future emperor, dressed in seedy dignity and always carrying a cudgel, Ratapoil, in Daumier's lithographs, stalked through France. The new Napoleon was elected president of the republic; Ratapoil led demonstrations for the empire. He promised all things to all men. He skulked around the edges of the government. He created images of glory and, like Macaire, he specialized in creating a demand.

He succeeded. The republic became again an empire. Laws again were passed to control the insolence of the press and Daumier again shifted his attention to the whole spectacle of Parisian life.

Daumier noted the opening rounds of the battle that still goes on as to whether photography is art. He went to the theater and always looked more searchingly at the audience than at the stage. He went to the art gallery and ignored the pictures, watching instead the effects of Manet's *Olympia* upon the viewers and those of a critic on the artists. Throughout the middle sixties, Daumier's crayon was never still, echoing in its movements the nervous rhythm of the capital of the second empire. With sardonic humor, the artist staked out the classic subjects of journalist cartoonists ever since and he also ventured into territory his successors have generally stayed clear of. Like everyone in Europe, Daumier became aware of the warlike intentions of Bismarck's Prussia. He saw, too, the use being made of war on the Paris stock exchange. In the last years before the Franco-Prussian War, Daumier drew incessantly against the coming danger. He saw the "European Equilibrium" precariously maintained on bayonets. He drew a vision of all the wars since his time in *The Dream of the Inventor of the Needle Gun*, with everybody dead except the grinning figure of the man of military science.

Daumier's warnings had never saved France before and they did not now. The empire killed itself upon the Prussian bayonets as it had killed the republic beneath the cudgels of Ratapoil. Daumier, old before his years, drew one last great political lithograph, employing, for almost the first time, the stock symbolism of poetry and rhetoric: the great oak is shattered by the

228.

HONORÉ DAUMIER,
Odysseus and Penelope.
Lithograph, 1842.

229.

HONORÉ DAUMIER,
*The dream of the inventor
of the needle gun.*
Lithopragh, 1866.

230.

HONORÉ DAUMIER,
Poor France!
Lithograph, 1871.

ACTUALITÉS. 213

Le reve de l'inventeur du fusil à aiguilles,
le jour de la Toussaint

ACTUALITÉS 299

Pauvre France!... le tronc est foudroyé, mais les racines tiennent bon!

storm and bent by the wind, but there is a rift in the clouds and there are fresh leaves on the single branch. *Poor France*, the title runs, *The trunk is blasted, but the roots still hold!*

All his life Honoré Daumier fought a losing battle for the republic. All his life he worked hard, sometimes having as many as eight lithographic stones at once laid out around a table. All his life he studied mankind and, with brilliant crayon, tried to get mankind to join him in this study. Daumier was devoted to industry, to freedom, to honesty. In addition, he was a genius. In his last years the artist reaped the reward of these virtues, namely, poverty. In the first years of the third republic, which preserved and gave new impetus to many of the character traits of the last kingdom and the second empire, Daumier found himself destitute. Through the kindness of an artist friend, Daumier was given a roof over his head for his last few years.

The whole period of his life and the period since his death have both been great ones for artists coming down from Mount Sinai with the single definitive word on what must be done in art. Daumier never ascended Sinai, or, if he did, he kept quiet about any universal laws entrusted to his care. He did say one thing, but it is such a general statement that it could apply to all trades. Yet, it is personal enough to stand as the artist's word on his work. In a dedication to a friend, Daumier once wrote, simply, "It is necessary to be of one's time."

Rouault

Rouault

The Franco-Prussian War and its aftermath of a brief, bitter civil war in Paris made up the last tragedy Daumier witnessed in France. During that upheaval and shedding of blood, indeed, according to legend, during an artillery barrage directed by the French government against a workers' quarter in Paris, there was born in the target area the spiritual successor of Daumier, Georges Rouault.

Birth in such a place at such a time was appropriate to the works of Georges Rouault. He was, on the one hand, a great religious artist, probably the greatest the twentieth century knew throughout its first sixty years. In his paintings and prints the spirit of the Christian faith returned to art after a long absence. But at the same time, Rouault was as keenly aware as Daumier and Goya of a fundamental injustice in a social system based on the hard work and insecurity of the many and dedicated to the vulgar luxury of the few. From the bringing together of those two often opposed beliefs comes much of the sheer power of the great black and white prints of Rouault.

For the two notions have been in violent opposition at many times in European history and never more violently than throughout the century of Daumier and of Rouault's youth. Once the Christian Church came up out of the catacombs of the declining Roman Empire, it found itself in alliance with whatever combination of wealth and power was ruling in the succeeding ages. From time to time – as in the gradual transformation of Roman slavery into medieval serfdom – the influence of Christianity was able to moderate the natural appetite of rulers for the exploitation of the ruled. But generally the alliance between throne and altar was an essential part of churchmanship, in any church in any century. The saints, it should be remembered, were not particularly influenced by the alliance, but the management of the churches was almost never influenced by the saints. Thus it happened that anyone interested in improving the lot of the poor was almost forced to oppose religion in Europe. Similarly the church, any church, tended to oppose any effort at social justice as a threat to divinely instituted private property. Thus it was entirely natural that Goya should have been anticlerical and that the Spanish Inquisition should have been anti-Goya; that Daumier should have lumped the monks and the bishops of France along with such enemies of freedom as Ratapoil and Louis-Philippe; that Van Gogh, preaching the gospel among the exploited coal miners of Holland, should have incurred the distrust and opposition of his church.

The last century has seen a vast change in that historic churchly attitude. A measure of the change is the active backing that the major American denominations give to social legislation; another is the active concern many clergymen take with labor unions,

231.
GEORGES ROUAULT, 1871-1958,
Miserere (plate 1):
Have mercy upon me God,
according to Thy great mercy.
Aquatint, etching, heliogravure
and other methods,
1914-1927, pub. 1948.

232.
GEORGES ROUAULT,
Miserere (plate 2):
Jesus reviled...

233.
GEORGES ROUAULT,
Miserere (plate 6):
Are we not convicts?

which, not too long ago, were denounced from the pulpit as wicked conspiracies of the indolent against the industrious. In Rouault's France, a measure of the change was the revolutionary priest-worker movement in the years following World War II. When Rouault was a youth, an art student, a young painter in Paris, that change was just beginning. It is by no means certain that Rouault's art was shaped by that new view of Christian reality which has transformed religion in the twentieth century. It seems entirely fair to conclude, however, that Rouault himself, in the example of his dedicated life and in the powerful message of his paintings and prints, has contributed greatly to the making of the new Christianity.

One reason for the rare combination of Christian faith and a passion for social justice may have been Rouault's working-class background. His father was a cabinetmaker employed by a piano factory. The boy himself, at fourteen, was apprenticed to a stained-glass maker. He grew to maturity with the deep habits of the French craftsman etched upon his character. When he decided to become a "fine" artist, at the age of twenty, he was already a craftsman who respected his materials and his tools by instinct. Rouault's growth was slow – as slow, in terms of a career, as was the growth, by accretion, of one of his thick, glowing paintings; or the growth, by the opposite process, of one of his rich, black prints. When still in his twenties, he was still doing run-of-the-mill religious paintings, of the kind made to induce intellectual slumber and still being made in Paris and elsewhere today. Then, around the turn of the century, something changed for Rouault. He became sensitively aware of the actual conditions of life in the poorer quarters of Paris. And he became aware that his own religious art would henceforth find its focus in the poor and oppressed of society.

He exhibited with the "Fauves" in the early years of the century, but it was clear from the first that any connection was really accidental. The Fauves – Matisse, Braque, Derain, Vlaminck – were interested in an explosion of color; Rouault was interested in an explosion of the human spirit. The Fauve association didn't last long; as a magnet for the young and a scandal for the old, it was speedily replaced by Cubism. Rouault went his solitary way on a path he pursued for over half a century. Until he was an old man Rouault never knew widespread worldly success. He worked slowly and steadily on everything he did. In mid-career he executed a series of fifty-eight prints that brilliantly summed up everything he had had to say in his painting, raised it all to a new profundity and contained virtually everything he was to do in painting in the thirty years of life left when the prints were made. The prints are those of the *Miserere*, which takes its title from

234.

GEORGES ROUAULT,
Miserere (plate 8):
Who does not wear a mask?

235.

GEORGES ROUAULT,
Miserere (plate 9):
*It happens, sometimes,
that the way is beautiful.*

the age-old cry of Jews and Christians, *"Have mercy on me, God, according to Thy great mercy."*

The circumstances of the making, printing and publishing of the *Miserere* plates are, like the artist's birth in war, appropriate to the content. In 1913 Rouault was discovered by a remarkable Parisian art dealer and publisher of de luxe editions, Ambroise Vollard. At a stroke he bought the entire contents of Rouault's studio, including some pictures the artist regarded as unfinished. Later on, Vollard set up a studio for Rouault in his own home so that the artist could complete such works. At about the same time, in 1917, he contracted with Rouault to take all of Rouault's production. Vollard gave Rouault a steady income and set him to printmaking for the de luxe editions of the Vollard firm. Among the projected books were two companion volumes, *Miserere* and *Guerre*, or *War*.

From first to last, in an effort to be helpful, in an effort at perfection, Vollard made the execution of *Miserere* a long agony to Rouault.

He had the artist start with drawings. From these Rouault made paintings and Vollard had the paintings transferred by heliogravure – a photographic process – to the largest sheets of copper that would fit in an etching press. The prints average twenty-one by eighteen inches. The intention was to facilitate Rouault's work as a printmaker. Instead, the artist found himself forced to obliterate most of the effects of the heliogravure. He engraved. He attacked portions of some plates with aquatint. He used drypoint, drawing the point along the copper to turn up a burr of rich, velvety darkness for the prints. He used the roulette and he sometimes applied etcher's acid directly to a plate with a brush. Technically the results are among the most fascinating examples of the printmaker's art, but the patient, experimenting, painstaking technique is completely a part of the patiently sought and found spiritual revelation.

Rouault conceived the idea of *Miserere* and *Guerre* in the first year of World War I. He was forty-three. Most of the drawings were done in the course of the war. For five years, from 1922 to 1927, he worked on the plates, in agony, exhaustion and triumph, passing from one aspect to another of man's hard lot on earth, of his salvation in Christ and of the identification between the exploited and murdered of all times and the exploited and murdered on Calvary. In 1927 the fifty-eight completed plates were printed in an edition of 450 copies, and the plates, by Vollard's direction, were canceled. Still publication was delayed. Vollard intended the prints to be accompanied by a religious text to be written by André Saurès. The text was never written. *Miserere et Guerre*, as the series was now called, was never published. Vollard died in the year that war came again to Europe, 1939.

236.

GEORGES ROUAULT,
Miserere (plate 10):
*In the old distinct
of long-suffering.*

237.

GEORGES ROUAULT,
Miserere (plate 11):
*Tomorrow will be beautiful
said the shipwrecked man...*

238.

GEORGES ROUAULT,
Miserere (plate 13):
*It would be
so sweet to love.*

After the war Rouault brought suit against the heirs of Vollard to establish his artist's rights in works of his possessed by the dealer's estate. He won the suit, establishing a legal precedent for all artists, and, in the presence of witnesses, burned over three hundred of the paintings restored to him. The same year, 1948, at last saw the publication of the *Miserere*, with one-line captions written by the artist. Rouault was sixty-seven. The whole of his middle age had passed between the idea and the public reality. But the whole of the *Miserere* had been conceived and created without reference to any of the art fashions that Paris had generated in the intervening years. In the post-World War II scene, the plates were as pertinent to man's fate as ever. In his old age the artist received the recognition of museums and the general public. Large exhibitions of his work were held in Europe, America and Japan. He was decorated by governments and knighted by the pope. When he died, in 1958, he was given a state funeral.

Miserere opens with the peace of death and the agony of dying. The title plate resembles some ancient funerary monument, stone marked by many weathers, crossed branches, face of an angel carved in low relief. Then, in the bottom half, the surface of the stone opens to reveal the bowed head of Christ awaiting the blows against the sketched landscape of suffering that is the authentic Rouault country. In the second plate, *Jesus reviled*, we have passed through the death monument into that country, closer to the bent head. The glowering sky is a gray background to the deep black of Christ's thorn-pressed head; His hair in turn is foil to the ghostly white areas in the face. The land behind is a simple group of heavy strokes.

From Christ wounded, Rouault passes to a wanderer on the earth and a figure sitting alone and in despair, helpless against the snares of life. The artist then presents one of the great sequences of the *Miserere*, a self-contained commentary on one of the major themes of the series. Against a scratched gray sky, a dark horizon, a humble home, a waiting mother and child, appears the stretched figure of a man, hands as if bound together, head thrown back in the inarticulate hope of an end to suffering. *Are we not convicts?* asks Rouault, and replies, *We think ourselves kings*, as the title of a crowned, robed, bejeweled man, whose eyes and teeth shine with the glint of madness. The convict and the king are followed by a clown. The movement of the three is as swift and as inexorable as classical dialectic: thesis of agony; antithesis of egomania; synthesis of pity and despair which nevertheless endures. The clown's face is twisted as his head is bent to one side. The deep shadows on either side are the marks of erosion in copper and in life. The light gleams on the forehead, elsewhere it fades into shadow. One eye is round like a target easily hit; the other is

239.

GEORGES ROUAULT,
Miserere (plate 15):
On lips that were fresh,
the taste of gall.

240.

GEORGES ROUAULT,
Miserere (plate 16):
The well-bred lady thinks
she has a reserved seat in heaven.

241.

GEORGES ROUAULT,
Miserere (plate 20):
Under a Jesus
forgotten on a cross.

242.

GEORGES ROUAULT,
Miserere (plate 23):
Lonely Street.

243.

GEORGES ROUAULT,
Miserere (plate 31):
"Love one another."

244.

GEORGES ROUAULT,
Miserere (plate 35):
*"Jesus will be
in agony until the end
of the world."*

cracked all the way across. Beneath this sad clown is Rouault's question, *Who does not wear a mask?*

The scene changes to a calm lakeside with a few figures, a boat, undisturbed waters, a sky brushed serenely with fading light: *It happens, sometimes, that the way is beautiful.* Again the scene changes, now to a working-class area of Paris, like Belleville, where Rouault was born in war. There are humble buildings, humble people, a bare tree, a child, a mother with her infant, the graceful line of her head and back contrasting with the stiff verticals of houses and tree. We are, Rouault announces, *in the old district of long-suffering.* Again the scene changes. Nervous black lines leap across the glowing sky. The horizon is formed by heavy seas. Something – a mast, a tree, pure fate – cuts across the scene and hangs heavy over the head of the man whose arm is raised and whose eyes are cast toward the sunset: *Tomorrow will be beautiful, said the shipwrecked man.*

Next comes a suite of women, beginning with a mother and child. They have already appeared in the background of the convict and as residents of the old district of long-suffering. Now they are presented by themselves. The relations of light and dark and especially the swinging curves of their forms present an ideal against which the bitter realities are measured. *It would be,* says Rouault, using the subjunctive of unfulfilled longing, *It would be so sweet to love.* There is a young prostitute, big-eyed, dumb as a sheep led to slaughter; another prostitute follows, head high, cheekbones and shoulder bones thrusting against the skin as if to break it. The light from below gives the girl a look of suffering past endurance yet endured to the edge of existence: *On lips that were fresh, the taste of gall.* In the next, *The well-bred lady thinks she has a reserved seat in heaven*, the smooth lines of her hair complement the smooth pale planes of her face. Her eyelids are decorously lowered, her lips are pressed together against the taste of gall, or the taste of life.

There are other landscapes, other callings, other betrayals, all taking place *under a Jesus forgotten on a cross.* The body is shaped to fit that cross and is pitifully thin against the heavy blackness of the upright. Behind that black stretches the seared land. Somewhere near the center of Rouault's landscape is the rundown, quiet neighborhood of *Lonely Street.* Darkness of sky matches encroaching shadow at the bottom of the picture. Between these two is the rushing perspective of the street, the bone-white of the houses, the streak of light along the sidewalk, everything else in black or gray. There are no doors, no windows, just black openings like blind eyes. Separate figures stand near each other halfway up the street. The walls of the buildings are pitted as if with some disease of childhood. Where the sides of the street come together, where Lonely Street approaches the van-

245.

GEORGES ROUAULT,
Miserere (plate 34):
*"Even the ruins
have been destroyed."*

246.

GEORGES ROUAULT,
Miserere (plate 38):
*The Chinese, they say,
invented gun powder,
made us a gift of it.*

247.

GEORGES ROUAULT,
Miserere (plate 40):
Face to face...

ishing point of perspective, there is no vanishing, only a great black stroke, like the shadow of a gibbet, that bars the way and closes all doors out from solitude.

Toward the end of what was planned as the first book, the *Miserere* proper, that gaunt body appears once more against the black block of the cross. There is still the suggestion of fragile flesh and bones stretched upon a rack to fit the ordained space. But now along with that, are the curves and the coming and going of light and gentle dark that Rouault earlier introduced in the figures of the mothers and their children. The agony and the hope of love have come together. The title is the prayer of Christ for man, recorded by St. John: "*Love one another.*"

What was to have been the title plate for the second book, *Guerre*, repeats the form established in the *Miserere* plate. But now the space above is occupied by the face of Christ as imprinted on the veil with which Veronica wiped the tortured face on the way to death. The space below is occupied by death itself, not in a landscape, but simply in a shallow niche. The title is "*Even the ruins have been destroyed.*" This is followed by a close-up of the racked torso of Christ. The head is bowed, the arms are almost straight up beneath the weight of the body. The frame cuts off the figure just above the elbows and just at the groin, so that the effect is of a moment lifted out of a viewing sequence from top to bottom. Beneath the picture is a thought from Pascal: "*Jesus will be in agony until the end of the world.*" Then death, as the age-old skeleton, makes his appearance; there is the suggestion of an ancient battlefield and then the surprising apparition of a Chinese scholar. He sits before an arch, beside a globelike vessel. The yin and yang of affirmative and negative – or life and death – are in an emblem on his chest; his hand is on his cheek; he stares vacantly into space, perhaps towards the Western world: *Chinese, they say, invented gunpowder, made us a gift of it.*

The citizen comes *Face to face* with war not as death erupting on battlefields, but as a well-fed bureaucrat – medical examiner or conscript officer – juxtaposed with the citizen's own exposed, naked and thin body. To woman, *War hated by mothers* brings the thought of Horace, *We must die, we and all that is ours.* The scene broadens to another landscape. From the whitened buildings, flame and smoke mount and cross the shadow line between earth and sky. The foreground, hollowed out by strokes of the brush, has its hollows filled by sacklike figures, soldiers resting or soldiers dead. At the horizon the sky is white, but it darkens above and the darkness surrounds the reclining figures. Rouault cries, *My sweet country, where are you?*

Death is everywhere, in the field, at home, attended by angels, attended by none. There is a pair of sad, globular faces hovering over a body stretched upon the earth: *In the wine-press, the grape*

248.

GEORGES ROUAULT,
Miserere (plate 44):
*My sweet country,
where are you?*

249.

GEORGES ROUAULT,
Miserere (plate 48):
*In the wine-press,
the grape was crushed.*

250.

GEORGES ROUAULT,
Miserere (plate 51):
*Far from the smile
of Rheims.*

251.

GEORGES ROUAULT,
Miserere (plate 52):
The law is hard,
but it is the law.

252.

GEORGES ROUAULT,
Miserere (plate 54):
"Arise, you dead!"

253.

GEORGES ROUAULT,
Miserere (plate 55):
Sometimes a blind
man has consoled the seeing.

was crushed. There is the face of a German soldier, the Iron Cross at his neck, the spectacles of German culture and scholarship slipping down his nose, a little frightened, a little ridiculous, yet three times in Rouault's life this German soldier was the terror of Europe and especially of France. Next to this soldier is a man of authority. Into his face are etched and carved the hard deep lines of justice and the lines no less hard of acceptance of what must be borne: *The law is hard, but it is the law.*

War, in this second half of the *Miserere*, comes to seem the natural, inevitable condition of life in the world that prints look upon. Toward the end there appears an image that takes us all the way back to the beginning of printmaking in Europe. Three skeletons mount into the air from the earth heaped up on their graves. The stones are set aside and the death figures walk in an ungainly way forward. The first wears an old campaign hat and raises his arm so that the whole picture space is spanned by the dead bones. Upon the distant horizon cemetery crosses are silhouetted against the dawn. *"Arise ye dead!"* is the title. Rouault has changed the meaning of the ancient image. It is the dead who rise in judgment. The hope of peace, the hope of justice are present in the immediately following plate. Two men walk forward before a stark low landscape and sky with the texture of a burial stone. One looks up with great black holes for eyes. The other, lids lowered, holds his companion's elbow and walks with head bowed. *Sometimes a blind man has consoled the seeing.*

The series ends as it began, with the figure of Christ. Again the body is stretched upon a cross and all the torture, all the suffering, all the blindness and loneliness, all the wish for love and the fact of war, all that has gone before is in the body and in the text from St. Paul: *"Obedient unto death, and to death on the cross."*

The last plate brings us again to the image on Veronica's veil, the print of the face of Christ caught by a gesture of compassion. Here are the marks of war and of a society that expresses itself in war. All the complex surfaces of the series are resolved in the simple juxtaposition of light against dark in succeeding rough frames moving toward the flat deep black of the bloodstained head. Rouault concludes with the prophecy of Isaias: *It is by his wounds that we are healed.*

254.
GEORGES ROUAULT,
Miserere (plate 57):
*"Obedient unto death
and to death on the cross."*

255.
GEORGES ROUAULT,
Miserere (plate 58):
*"It is by his wounds
that we are healed."*

War is the great subject of twentieth-century printmaking for the same reason that landscape was the great subject for nineteenth-century American painting: there's so much of it around. In France, Rouault was almost alone in creating a major work on the century's major activity; French art generally in the twentieth century became increasingly concerned with the discovery and solution of technical problems, with the construction of increasingly pure relationships of form and color. But on the other side of the Rhine, a whole generation of German artists paid close attention to war for the most understandable of reasons: war paid attention to them. As in France, painting held the central position in German art, but both the painters and the sculptors poured much energy into printmaking. One outstanding artist, Käthe Kollwitz, made prints her primary medium of expression, although she was also a sculptress of great power.

Kollwitz lived through the same wars that Rouault did, except that she didn't make it quite through the last and the biggest. She was born in 1867 in East Prussia, just a few years before Prussia created Germany in its own image. She died in Saxony in April, 1945, just as the Allied armies were crushing the last breath of life out of Hitler's vicious parody of Prussianism. Her younger son, Peter, was killed in action in the early days of World War I. Her first grandson, Peter, was killed in action in World War II. Her Berlin home, in which she lived for half a century and which held a vast collection of her drawings and prints, was destroyed by aerial bombing in 1943. She knew war well and made it the subject of her art.

She also knew the "long, long patience of the plundered poor," and the end of that patience. She was born in a strong socialist tradition and in an equally strong tradition of nonconformist Christianity. Of the two, socialism was probably more vital to her. Certainly her work shows more preoccupation with the vision of social revolution than with Christianity. Yet, in her letters and conversation she showed a deep interest in the Gospels. All her life she loved music and literature. She thought of Beethoven's *Ninth Symphony* as "pure socialism." Her other favorite was Bach's *Passion According to Saint Matthew.* She attended the theater frequently and read extensively, rereading Goethe throughout her life. In her early twenties she married Karl Kollwitz, a doctor who operated a clinic of socialized medicine in a working-class district of Berlin. It was in the nineties, while her sons were being born and raised through their earliest years, that Käthe Kollwitz made her first enduring achievements in printmaking. War, Christianity, socialism – all are caught up in her first and lasting theme, Motherhood.

Motherhood begins and ends her first print cycle on the social

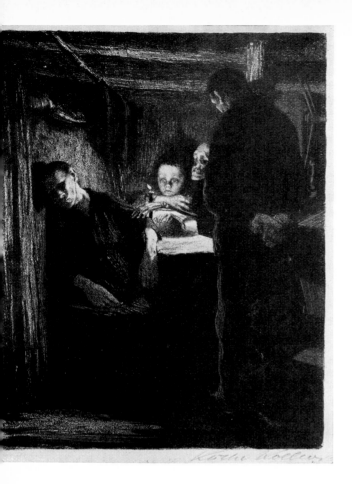

260.

KÄTHE KOLLWITZ, 1867-1945,
Weavers Cycle: Death.
Lithograph, 1897.

261.

KÄTHE KOLLWITZ,
Weavers Cycle: Conspiracy.
Etching, 1897.

262.

KÄTHE KOLLWITZ,
Weavers Cycle:
March of the Weavers.
Etching, 1897.

revolution, *The Weavers*. Inspired by the Gerhardt Hauptmann drama and based on a disastrous strike of 1840, the series portrays a futile attempt at social justice in the early days of modern industrialism.

The series begins with the lithograph, *Poverty*, the general condition against which the revolt began. An axis of light is established between the window and the mother and sick child in the foreground. Out of the surrounding darkness come the looms of the weavers and two other members of the family. The blank light of the window comes forward to rest upon the despairing mother and the blank face of the infant. The second plate, also a lithograph, is *Death*, whose bony hand reaches between husband and child to pluck the sleeve of the worn-out mother. Again the dark masses weigh heavily on every part of the picture. The husband's form is barely distinguishable from the general gloom. The light on the ceiling beams and wall only increases their grainy weight. All this weight presses down on the woman and we feel no incongruity at all between the allegorical skeleton of Death and the grim realism of the setting and the people.

Conspiracy, the third plate, is an etching. Consequently, as the exploited and oppressed workers begin to plan for light, the very darkness of their tavern headquarters is made of cross hatching, the mixture of light with darkness. The light on the wall, the light on the floor, the light on the table surround and give hope to the huddled, whispering bodies of the conspirators.

In the next plate, the *March of the Weavers*, an etching, the light-dark values have been completely reversed from what they were early in the series. In the open air, en route, determined, armed with the tools of work and with persistent indignation, the weavers are seen in the play of light upon their faces and clothes as they walk through the light of air and ground. Kollwitz moves from face to face and each one is an individual portrait of oppression and rebellion. But the central figure is that of the woman with the sleeping child on her back. Head down, she marches with her men because there is nothing else to do, carries her child because there is no place to leave it. In plate five, *Riot*, also an etching, she and the others have arrived at their destination – the establishment of the owners. Again light predominates, but the light tones of the wall are as hard as the black iron of the gate. Neither will give an inch to the workers' attack. The classic weapon of city rebels is employed, the tearing up of cobblestones; but for all the urgency of the hands reaching and hands pulling, the little band looks feeble and powerless against the immobile strength of the wall and gate. On the right a woman, holding two children, expresses in every line of her body the tragic knowledge that the protest will fail and that it had to be made.

263.

KÄTHE KOLLWITZ,
Weavers Cycle: Riot.
Etching, 1897.

264.

KÄTHE KOLLWITZ,
Weavers Cycle: The End.
Etching and aquatint, 1898.

265.
KÄTHE KOLLWITZ,
Peasant War Cycle: Plowing.
Etching and aquatint, 1906.

266.
KÄTHE KOLLWITZ,
Peasant War Cycle:
Sharpening the Scythe.
Etching and soft ground, 1905.

267.

KÄTHE KOLLWITZ,
Peasant War Cycle: Outbreak.
Mixed technique including etching,
soft ground and aquatint, 1903.

268.

KÄTHE KOLLWITZ,
Peasant War Cycle:
After the Battle.
Etching and soft ground, 1907.

Etching and aquatint make the grainy light and deeply lined dark of the last scene, *The End*. The mother is at home, receiving the dead. The streaks of pure white, through the door and past her resigned face, suggest the flight of bullets, the traditional last answer to labor negotiations in the nineteenth century. The contour lines of the dead men's clothing is in heavy contrast to the light grain of floor and wall. The utter regularity of the lines of the loom are another contrast. The work will endure. The same kind of lines depict the dress of the woman. She, too, will endure.

The *Weavers* was publicly shown in the Berlin Art Exhibition of 1898. The jury wished to award it the gold medal of the show, but this was stopped by the Kaiser. Nevertheless the set announced the arrival of a new talent and won Kollwitz honors in Dresden and London.

In the first decade of the new century she completed her second cycle of social revolution, the *Peasant War*. Again, the subject came from German history. Early in the sixteenth century the German princes were quarreling with the German emperor over who had the first right to the labor of the peasants. The peasants themselves came up with the dangerous notion that they themselves had some rights in the question and attempted to establish those rights by arms. This subversive attempt united all the better elements of society – civil, ecclesiastical, imperial, princely, intellectual – in an educational slaughter of the rebels.

The pattern is much the same as in *The Weavers*: cause for revolt, preparation, attack and, skipping precisely the part – the battle – that a conventional historian would stress, the end in death and defeat. In the first plate, *Plowing*, the men pulling the plow are at once shackled to the plow, a part of the plow, and straining not only to pull the plow but to raise themselves up from the earth. Their tension is against both the weight of the plow and the low, level land. The two bodies are almost identical in posture, but one lets his head hang toward the earth, the other – the nearer member of the team – keeps his head up to take the light and to look ahead. The tension in *Sharpening the Scythe* is all interior. The woman's hand, the blade, the stone, her eye, pick up the plowman's look to the light. The great variety of texture, achieved by soft ground etching, effectively underscores the daily degradation of a peasant's life. The two tensions combine in the *Fight in Castle Armory*. The strain of the plowmen now surges up the stairs, out of the light of day into the darkness of weapons and fortifications held by the rulers. The strain of the scythe sharpener is in the faces pressing forward and in the points of weapons seized. The movement continues and reaches a crescendo in *Outbreak*. The rebel peasants are formed in a shrieking wedge, hurling themselves, with clumsy

269.
KÄTHE KOLLWITZ,
Peasant War Cycle: The Prisoners.
Etching and soft ground, 1908.

steps, against the law of might. The mother in the foreground urges them on with hands raised as a priestess invoking the sacred act of protest. Her body is at once part of the attack and a counterpoise to the attack.

Then Kollwitz simply passes over the joining of the issue, the bloody events in which the ancient aristocracy of soldiers and hunters proved itself capable of fighting off the people on whose labor it had lived so long. In *After the Battle*, the forms are quiet; the sky comes down to the level horizon; the earth shades from distant light to close dark. Within that dark, the forms become visible and their quiet is death. The monumental form of the woman breaks the pale light of the sky, as the light of her shaded lamp breaks the darkness of death and she seeks her own. Everything is misted over by darkness or distance except her gnarled, work-worn hand. In the next and last plate, *The Prisoners*, the dramatic isolation of the searching mother is replaced and softened by the bound figures of the captive peasants, awaiting their fate in sure knowledge of what is coming but in stolid determination that the struggle will be renewed.

The reality drawn and etched by Käthe Kollwitz and rejected by both the Kaiser and the Empress, came to Germany in full flood with the end of the war and the disorders of peace. The only advantage the defeat gave the Germans was that at least the Kaiser was gone. Like her countrymen, Kollwitz profited from the imperial departure. In the republic she was elected to the academy, which gave her a studio and the title of "professor."

In those years of postwar horror in central Europe, Käthe Kollwitz responded to appeals from all sources; much of her work is in the form of lithographic posters asking for food for children or urging permanent peace. In 1923 she did another powerful cycle of prints. The theme was *War*; the medium was the woodcut. In the monumental forms of this series, we are reminded that she was also a sculptor, and was, at that time, struggling with a sculptured memorial to her son. The figures of *The Parents* or the *Widow I* might have been cut in three dimensions at life size. Since the wood left uncut is the wood that prints, Kollwitz reversed the normal procedure of the woodcut throughout the series. The opening plate, *The Sacrifice*, recalling her own pride as the mother of German soldiers, is so designed that the form of the mother is cut into the wood rather than cut away from it. This is also true of the *Parents* and *Widow I* and is carried to its extreme in the final block, *The People*. The mute darkness is unbroken save by the purposeful knife of the artist and the consequent appearance of a face, a hand, a child protected, a mother wary.

War was the great subject in Germany in 1923, for its consequences were everywhere and were portrayed by poets, play-

270.
KÄTHE KOLLWITZ,
War Cycle: The Sacrifice.
Woodcut, 1923.

271.
KÄTHE KOLLWITZ,
War Cycle: The Widow I.
Woodcut, 1923.

272.
KÄTHE KOLLWITZ,
War Cycle: The Parents.
Woodcut, 1923.

273.
KÄTHE KOLLWITZ,
War Cycle: The People.
Woodcut, 1923.

274.
KÄTHE KOLLWITZ,
Death Cycle: Woman Welcoming Death.
Lithograph, 1934-35.

wrights, novelists, and painters. In her woodcuts, Kollwitz managed the considerable feat of composing a powerful protest against war and the expression of its horror without a soldier, a gun, a battle, a death. There is only love bereaved.

The artist's period of official acceptance came late and did not last long. In 1933 Hitler became chancellor of Germany and work by Kollwitz was removed from public exhibition and forbidden to be handled by dealers. The artist herself lost her academy studio. After 1935 she did few more prints but in that year she completed her last great series, *Death*.

The eight lithographs reveal total mastery of the medium she once characterized by saying, "There is no technique, it is all essentials." To the essentials she clings; every stroke of the crayon counts. Settings are dispensed with. Emotion is created with the rhythm of the strokes and the grain of the print. The series opens with the calm statement of *Woman Welcoming Death*. There is a vagueness of outline here and there, but how sharply the profile of the welcoming face stands against the white. The children shrink from death and the mother at once protects them and offers her hand to the visitor.

There follow two more or less public ways of death, *In the Water*, and *On the Highway*; two completely different effects of the crayon give two related modes of death. The water mingles with the figures, all is grainy, the bodies a little more so than the surrounding water. The figure of *Death on the Highway* is very distinct and composed of many strokes of the crayon, each separate like the repeated blows of violent death. Then there is nothing but swooping line as *Death Reaches for a Woman*. The violence continues in *Death as a Friend*; this frantic clutch is different from the calm of the first plate. *Death with Girl in Lap* is once more pity for the relief the girl shows in this encounter. *Death Swoops* is again violent as one mood, one response to the one common fact of experience succeeds another and is succeeded in turn. This fluctuating response is resolved in the pure serenity of line and tone in the final stone, *The Call of Death*. The old woman looks up, as if from her reading or her work, to find the long-expected touch upon her shoulder. With total economy, the face comes out of the shadow. With dynamic balance, the upward diagonal toward death is stabilized by the strong vertical of a face and an arm.

Käthe Kollwitz was that rarest of creatures, an authentic woman artist. More, she was an artist of womanhood and an artist in womanhood. She created a rich life for her children and shared the dedication of her husband. It was within that domestic milieu that the art of Käthe Kollwitz attained its growth. The beginnings are recorded in an early etching, *Self Portrait at the Table*. It is the deep experience of life that forms the lithographic *Self Por-*

275.

KÄTHE KOLLWITZ,
Death Cycle:
Death in the Water.
Lithograph, 1934-5.

276.

KÄTHE KOLLWITZ,
Death Cycle:
Death Upon the Highway.
Lithograph, 1934-5.

277.
KÄTHE KOLLWITZ,
Death Cycle:
Death Reaches for a Woman.
Lithograph, 1934.

278.
KÄTHE KOLLWITZ,
Death Cycle:
Death as a Friend.
Lithograph, 1934-5.

279.
KÄTHE KOLLWITZ,
Death Cycle:
Death with Girl in Lap.
Lithograph, 1934-5.

trait of 1924 and the face of suffering endured and truth still sought in the lithograph of ten years later.

Someone once noted wisely that the histories of wars are all written by the victors. Käthe Kollwitz wrote a history of war from the point of view of the always vanquished. Confronted by the madness of her century, she twice compressed all that she wished to say to a single cry – *Seed Corn Must Not Be Ground*. The first time was in response to a World War I patriotic proposal for one final draft of schoolboys as the Western Front was cracking. The second time was one war later, as Americans in Italy found their prisoners to be twelve-year-olds in uniform.

A week before her death she wrote in a letter, "The war accompanies me to the end."

Chapter Thirteen

Printmaking Today

Printmaking Today

Kollwitz wasn't alone in German printmaking of the early twentieth century. German art in general was vital and a number of conditions made Germany a more fruitful climate for biting prints than almost anywhere else. For one thing, the art life there was closely associated with political life. Artists were intimately aware of what was going on from the coming of World War I to the coming of Hitler. They cared deeply about what was going on and a good deal of what was going on got into their art. In Paris, on the contrary, the whole art of the first half of the century concerned itself almost exclusively with art itself. Also, German art never became really fashionable, even in Germany, until long after most of the artists had ceased to live in Germany.

The question of subject matter and the related question of an artist's commitment, in his art, to some program or position outside his art, are both very difficult. No one needs to be told that it isn't the subject that matters. The old song says quite correctly that, "It ain't what you do, it's the way that you do it." Moreover, the attics of the world and the basements of all the museums are filled with pictures painted, prized and purchased chiefly because the subject matter was important or the views of the artist very popular. From the truth of these observations it is easy to conclude that the existence of nonartistic subject matter or the holding of nonartistic views are actually detrimental to art. There are observers of the art scene who honestly feel that Käthe Kollwitz was no artist, but simply a propagandist for the widely held viewpoint that it is too bad that mothers' children have to die in war. Oddly enough that judgment is rarely made of, for example, Michelangelo. No one dismisses him as merely a religious propagandist, albeit a powerful one.

He is saved from this fate by a number of other considerations, chief among which is the belief that he actually lay on his back under the Sistine Ceiling for four years because he was fascinated by the technical problems of the nude male body represented in fresco painting.

It seems more likely, much more likely, that Michelangelo really did believe very deeply in the scripture he was portraying and what's more believed in it not only as a group of historic events and persons, but as a cause in the souls of men, which cause could be furthered by such things as fresco painting. The notion of Michelangelo as exclusively interested in problems of form seems to be a backward projection of late nineteenth- and early twentieth-century attitudes. The person knowledgeable in art in that recent epoch couldn't quite take the Book of Genesis seriously – it had all been disproved by the Neanderthal Man. Therefore he couldn't imagine Michelangelo taking it seriously either. Since, on the other hand, such an art-knowledgeable person was intensely interested in such technical questions as anatomy in art, it

284.
EMIL NOLDE, 1867-1956,
Saul and David.
Etching, 1911.

followed naturally that Michelangelo, who had certainly attacked and solved such problems, was interested in them to the exclusion of everything else. The Sistine Ceiling was really a titanic joke in which the artist got the pope to finance his extensive experiments in anatomy.

A similar process may be observed at work over the identity of Shakespeare. The complex structure of his plays, in everything from main action to figures of speech, offers such a stimulating field for exegesis that it is assumed he must have been a scholarly exegete himself, an Elizabethan Ph.D. candidate rather than a practical theater man writing for a deadline. Hence the historical Shakespeare, a practical theater man, is discarded as unlikely, and the authorship of the plays attributed to, among others, Francis Bacon, a highly talented exegete. Actually, according to at least one practical theater man, "Francis Bacon" was a name and a literary personality invented by Christopher Marlowe as a convenience when hiding from his creditors.

Unlike Michelangelo's, the faith of Käthe Kollwitz is on the whole now shared very widely – particularly, perhaps, by people interested in art. We're all socialists nowadays. The Conservatives in England can think of nothing more conservative to promise than more efficient administration of socialist enterprises. So it goes everywhere. Yesterday's revolution is today's way of the world and that probably explains the objections to the social content in the art of Kollwitz and other twentieth-century printmakers. The faith seems real, therefore the art seems false. When, in a generation or so, society has passed beyond socialism, art purists, no longer socialist in their convictions, will be able to accept the art of Käthe Kollwitz as having employed the naïve faith of our fathers as a plausible occasion for experiments in lithographic crayon. In the meantime, to the nonpurist, all things may be art, even those in which the artist believed.

Emil Nolde was a contemporary of Kollwitz, creator of a large body of highly colored, exultant paintings in oil and water color. His prints often express the opposite extreme of human emotion, as in the etching, *Saul and David*. The young harpist is present most strongly in his hand on the harp, fingers open. Saul's hand clutches the javelin he is shortly to throw at his court musician and successor. In the darkness the face of David shines, not so much inscrutable in the darkness as simply unformed. Saul's face is completely formed and all the etched marks on his gown contribute to the pity evoked by the old man, long decayed in power, unable to hear the music for itself.

Elsewhere in the north of Europe, a Norwegian, Edvard Munch, made visible in his paintings the neuroses and hysteria of the age. His *The Cry*, a lithograph based on a painting, is a classic image of extreme emotion expressed directly. The central figure's

285.
EDVARD MUNCH, 1863-1944,
The Cry.
Lithograph, 1893.

286.
OTTO DIX, b. 1891,
Wounded, Fall, 1916, Bapaume.
Etching and Aquatint, 1924.

287.

GEORGE GROSZ, 1893-1959,
Christmas Eve.
Lithograph, 1921.

288.
PABLO PICASSO, b. 1881,
The Frugal Repast.
Etching on zinc, 1904.

hands and face record the scream, but the pervading causes of the scream and its continuing echo are expressed in the swirling lines, including those on the body and the swift perspective of the promenade railing. The lines of the sky and the water could almost pass for a picture of sound waves. *The Cry* is also a superb illustration of the flexibility of a lithograph, not because the artist wished to pretend he was using the more difficult medium, of woodcut but because such strong, dominant lines, with their suggestion of carving, were perfectly suited to the subject.

Another contemporary of Kollwitz was her friend, the sculptor, Ernst Barlach. In lithographs and especially woodcuts, Barlach brought the rare combination of monumentality and individuality that distinguishes his sculpture. *God Over the City* has the look of a monumental, idealized image of an old religious conception, the presence of God in all lives. Much of the monumental effect comes from the juxtaposing of the diagonal, soaring form of God against the Gothic verticals of the city and from heightening that contrast by making the city chiefly black on white, God's figure chiefly white on black. At the very heart of this monumental concept, however, is the face of God, with a definite personality, that of a powerful but patient and extremely skeptical observer. This individuality, in fact, flows all through the figure, the hands, the feet, even the folds of the robe.

Two aspects of the effects of World War I on German art may be seen in the prints by Otto Dix and George Grosz. In *Wounded*, Dix created, in etching and aquatint, a horrifying image of the individual soldier lost and stricken in the nightmare of modern warfare. The bitten-into quality of the surroundings, the scratches on the skin and uniform of the soldier, both testify to the nature of the world from which the soldier recoils into madness. Grosz in some ways always maintained more control over his response to the German madness and its aftermath. His disgust and revulsion were tempered by cool irony, as in *Christmas Eve*, where the delicate line accents the flabby forms, and the well-known hymn and religious sentiment in general are pressed into the service of bourgeois comfort.

The whole of German art, including printmaking, was cut off as if with a knife by the active hostility of the Nazi government in the 1930s. Decree followed decree, removing work by the vital German artists from exhibition and from public sale. The Nazis attempted to create a German art which would be the equivalent of the "socialist realism" created by the Soviet Union, but Hitler's great adventure of World War II put an end to his regime and to its art enterprise. The artistic community of the country was harassed and scattered. When the Nazi nightmare was over, many of the country's artists were dead or in exile. Continuity had been broken. The new generation of German artists for the most

289.
REGINALD MARSH, 1898-1954,
The Jungle.
Etching 1931.

290.
JOHN SLOAN, 1871-1951,
Roofs, Summer Night.
Etching, 1926.

part accepted wholeheartedly the art-for-the-sake-of-art approach that had long predominated in Paris.

In Paris itself, at the very heart of a new, beautiful and aloof art stood an artist who was far from unconcerned with the quality of life around him. This was Pablo Picasso, the Spaniard who was the leading French artist for half a century. Picasso's own commitment to an art detached from all else has probably been exaggerated by his admirers. Certainly one of his greatest works, his painting, *Guernica*, is anything but unconcerned with what is going on in the world. And throughout some sixty years of incessant production in sculpture, painting and printmaking, there is, along with a frank fascination with the odd turns that can be given to form, a steady interest in the human condition. Except for the outrage in *Guernica* and related works, occasioned by the Civil War in Spain, Picasso's emotional attitude toward humanity seems to be one of wry compassion. The zinc etching, *Frugal Repast*, of 1904, is the very image of hunger and hard times borne with a kind of hopeless heroism.

The record of hard times, with or without hopeless heroism, occupied much of the effort in American printmaking up to and including World War II. Reginald Marsh's *Jungle* expresses one extreme form of such times. Less extreme is John Sloan's *Roofs, Summer Night*, in which the urban poor sacrifice privacy for air. The strength of the picture is in the shadowed mass of the rooftops opening up in perspective to scene after scene of the same subject. The rural aspect of the same general feeling is recorded by Thomas Hart Benton's lithograph, *In the Ozarks*. Direct attack on the evils of hard times was carried on by many American artists, many of whom drew for socially critical publications. William Gropper's *Sweatshop* not only records conditions in the pre-union garment industry, but makes its point of hopelessnesss as much by the over-all bareness of the scene, the line of operators, and such details as the hanging rack and the light fixture, as it does by the expressions on faces.

Social satire in a somewhat different sense was carried on not only by Peggy Bacon, whose *Patroness* is a superb example, but also by Adolf Dehn, who, like Daumier, had no reluctance to use the laugh as an aesthetic response. *Art Lovers* might well fit into the comment on the same subject initiated by Daumier. The figures are almost like members of a trained chorus in the dispositions of gesture and expression.

After World War II there has been, in Europe and America equally, a withdrawal from general human concerns on the part of artists, and printmakers have gone along with the rest. Printmakers, indeed, led the way. In the last years of the nineteenth century and the opening years of the twentieth, there was a high

291.
THOMAS HART BENTON, b. 1889,
In the Ozarks.
Lithograph, 1938.

292.
WILLIAM GROPPER, b. 1897,
Sweatshop.
Lithograph, bef. 1938.

293.
PEGGY BACON, b. 1895,
Patroness.
Lithograph, 1927.

294.
ADOLF DEHN, 1895,
Art Lovers.
Lithograph, 1934.

295.
GERSON LEIBER, b. 1921,
Under the El.
Intaglio, 1957.

print connoisseurship that concentrated on the deep appreciation of the technical qualities of etchings. Except for Whistler, the artists who enjoyed such admiration are now almost all forgotten, yet the basic attitude has moved into printmaking on a wider scale than ever before. Technical experiments, such as those of Stanley Hayter, are highly valued both by artists and collectors. Among whole group of printmakers, texture seems to have become an end in itself. Some lovely things are being produced; but, after all, lovely textures are being produced in men's suitings and in furniture upholstery, and there is more to art than textures.

As printmakers moved into technical studies, a number of other things were happening elsewhere to take the bite out of prints. One thing that happened was the use, in France, of prints as substitutes for paintings. Before the war, but especially since the war, large editions of color lithographs and serigraphs by name artists of the school of Paris have appeared on the market. In many cases these works are essentially reproductions of paintings made by skilled technicians and signed by the artist. Thus there has been repeated the history of the mezzotint in the eighteenth century, with the difference that purchasers of mezzotints were aware they were getting and indeed wanted to get reproductions of paintings by Reynolds and the rest, while the twentieth-century purchaser of Paris prints is often under the impression that he is getting an original work from the hand of the artist who signed the print.

Another thing that's happened is photography. Art still hasn't made up its mind about photography and nowhere is this indecision more evident than in the world of prints. Some museum print departments, for example, exhibit photographs, which, after all, are prints in the sense of exactly repeatable images. There are still very few collectors of photographs and, for that matter, very little existing machinery for the sale of photographic prints. But as long as photography is available, many print collectors, curators, and makers feel that it is superfluous for the print artist to make recognizable images, the theory apparently being that all visual art before the camera was limited to doing by hand what the camera does chemically.

A more profound effect of photography on printmaking is in the photomechanical reproduction of drawings. The political or social cartoonist today need be a draughtsman only. His drawing is reproduced in a line engraving that is made in a minute and is good for at least several million impressions.

The problem here is that such work has taken over talents that earlier would have used lithographs or engravings and hence could have been called printmakers, even if they only supplied drawings to craftsmen. The political cartoonist delivers his drawings not

296.

HERBLOCK, b. 1909,
Krushchev cartoon,
1961.

297.

MAURICIO LASANSKY, b. 1914,
Self-portrait.
Engraving, 1957.

298.

LEONARD BASKIN, b. 1922,
Man with Forsythia.
Wood engraving, 1953.

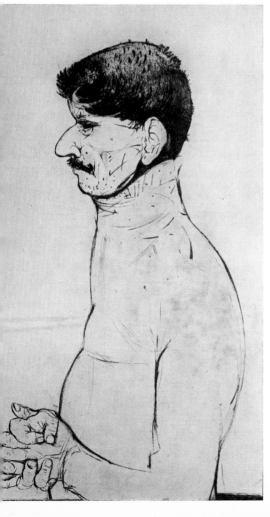

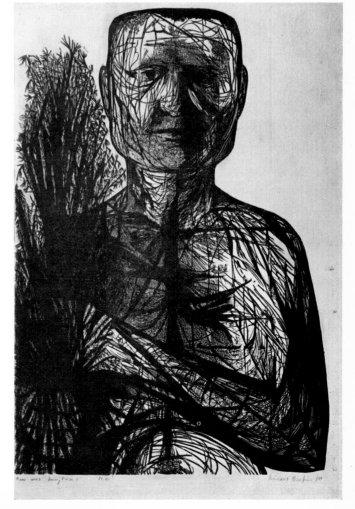

to a craftsman but to a machine, and therefore he cannot be recognized as a printmaker. All this has something to do with the theory of society developed by Thorstein Veblen. Drawings by cartoonists can be exhibited, but the printed cartoons themselves cannot, chiefly because anywhere from half a million to two million impressions of any one of them is likely to be in existence and may be bought for a nickel along with the news of the day. The same problem has existed in regard to Daumier. To this day you can pick up Daumier lithographs printed in the *Charivari* for a couple of dollars and therefore there has been an instinctive movement to hail Daumier as a sculptor and as a painter but not as a printmaker. In the work of men like Saul Steinberg, Bill Mauldin, and Herblock there is clearly evident the management of line and form and the rather skeptical point of view that have characterized so much of the world's great printmaking. None of the three will ever be accepted as a printmaker unless he starts doing by hand what is now so perfectly done for him by machine.

Despite all these considerations, there are a great many post-World War II printmakers who continue to be concerned with the human condition and to let their art be formed to some extent by that concern.

Gerson Leiber's *Under the 'El*, an intaglio print, uses the weight of the elevated structure to bear down on the isolated figure walking along beneath the girders. The weight is actually increased by not being expressed in a solid black. Not only is the structure open to the sky between the ties and gratings of the girders, but the girders themselves are richly decorated with bolts and struts throughout. The flat perspective of the structure suggests that the walker is moving toward a quiet extinction.

Among the best known American printmakers today are Mauricio Lasansky, Misch Kohn, Dean Meeker, and Leonard Baskin, who is also a sculptor. All have the quality expressed in the title of this book. Lasansky's intaglio *Self-Portrait* creates a person and a point of view with an honest line that culminates in head and hands. Baskin's *Man with Forsythia* uses the qualities of wood engraving to relate the nervous and blood systems of a man to the plant-cell system of the flowers he carries. Kohn's *Lion* is made of etching, engraving, and aquatint, and employs all three to improvise upon the decorative strength of the king of the beasts. Almost in passing, Kohn picks up the real values of the contemporary school of spontaneity in art and employs them to reveal more about the lion and about the experience of the lion by human eyes, brain, and printman's hand. Meeker's *Surgeon*, an etching, is an awesome image, suggesting, through the biting and cutting qualities of the medium, the similar qualities in the profession under consideration. The only substantial flat area in

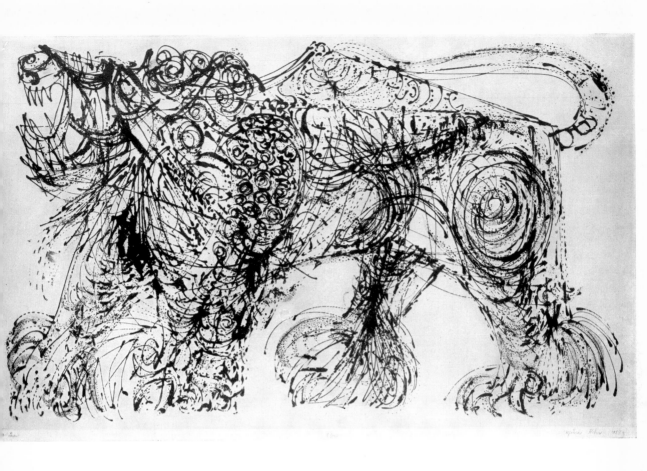

299.
MISCH KOHN, b. 1916,
Lion.
Etching, aquatint, engraving, 1957.

300.
DEAN MEEKER, b. 1921,
Surgeon.
Intaglio, 1957.

the print is that of the surgeon's hands which control all the points and blades on the table, all the shadow areas elsewhere.

One of the most important American printmakers and teachers of printmaking is Gabor Peterdi. His classes at Yale University have produced a young generation of extremely competent artists. His book, *Printmaking*, is a gold mine of method and experiment for both maker and viewer. Peterdi is noted in his own work chiefly for his effects in color. He can, seemingly, make it do anything he wants and there is often a pulsing loveliness to what he does make it do in combination with new textures. Yet Peterdi is capable of expression as classically biting as anything in the last four centuries. *Still Life in Germany*, a line engraving of 1946, has some of the bitter irony of Goya's mood in *I Saw This*, but where Goya, throughout the *Disasters,* used technique – aquatint – as a soft and subtle screen between reality and response, Peterdi pushes technique the other way. The clarity, the precision, even the elegance of line engraving all underline the ghastliness of the still life arrangement. That arrangement, in this medium, ironically recalls a long German tradition of close anatomical drawing. Memories of both Dürer and Grünewald are evoked to comment on their country. One of the achievements of the Nazis was to create a horror so complete that few artists have been able to go beyond the power of the camera's lens in depicting it. Peterdi is one of the few.

More formally experimental, Peterdi's 1957 print, *Massacre of the Innocents,* is a combination of etching and engraving heightened by color laid on with linoleum block. The look, obviously, has also changed. Yet the difference between the earlier print and the later is not so much that between realism and abstraction, as that between close-up and long view. The subject is the same. The means are freer, partly because the treatment of landscape is always freer than that of selected detail. The larger landscape of horror comes through powerfully in forms that suggests both bombers and great predatory birds. The thin lines establish planes that are at once the earth in perspective, the lines of tracer bullets and the meeting of planes to mark the spot of destruction. Color erupts like flame and the whole image is that of planned chaos, the total disorder that can only come from the attempt at total order.

It thus appears that while there is much stress on graphic experiment, following Hayter, the individual printmakers who emerge from the collective interest in texture are largely able to employ that interest for the traditional ends of the printmaker.

In the last few chapters of this book, those ends may have appeared to have something to do with the advance of socialism in the political and economic world. In the earlier chapters those ends may have appeared to have something to do with the advance of

301.

GABOR PETERDI, b. 1915,
Massacre of the Innocents.
Etching and engraving, 1957.

the Christian religion. Neither is the case. Religion and socialism have, if you like the word, "used" printmaking for their respective purposes, but printmaking has certainly used religion and socialism just as much. The use of both for the purposes of the print derives partly because both historically have created a widely held body of beliefs within which an artist can address himself to a large number of people, but even more because both religion and socialism are, from one point of view, criticism of the way things are; and it is criticism, in the widest sense, that seems to be the genius of printmaking.

The existence of the talent and the interest has been made clear, albeit rather sketchily compared to the wealth of material now being created in print studios. The material for the critical printmaker is nothing else but the mortal and venial sins of man and of man's institutions. A printmaker, such as Goya, may start out to record and protest human barbarity and finish by creating visual tragedy of the highest order. Whatever the beginnings and ends of individual printmakers, those mortal and venial sins of man and society remain his material. That material is never in short supply.

307.
GABOR PETERDI,
Still Life in Germany.
Line Engraving, 1947.

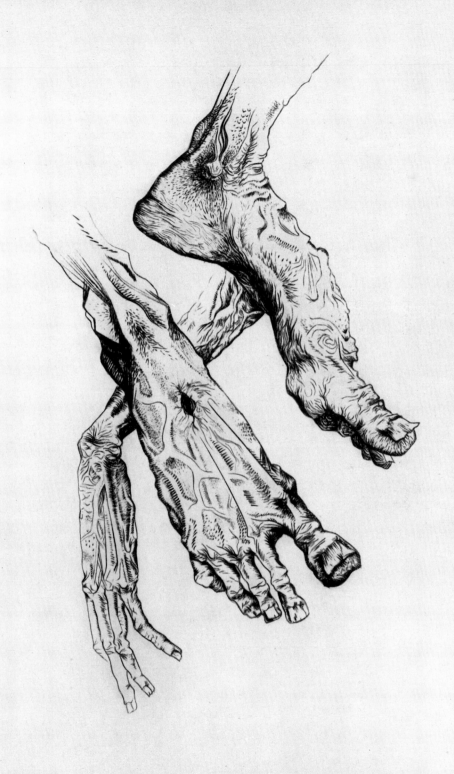

Bibliography

Chapter One: THE BITE

General Books on Print Making

HAAS, IRVING. *A Treasury of Great Prints.* New York: Barnes, 1956.

HIND, ARTHUR MAYGER. *A History of Engraving and Etching from the 15th Century to 1914.* London: Constable, 1923.

HOFMANN, WERNER. *Caricature.* New York: Crown, 1957.

KENNEDY GALLERIES. *Five Centuries of Fine Prints.* New York: Yearly catalogues, beginning 1960.

LONGSTREET, STEPHEN. *A Treasury of the World's Great Prints.* New York: Simon and Schuster, 1961.

SCHAB GALLERIES. *Graphic Arts of Five Centuries.* New York. Comprehensive catalogues.

ZIGROSSER, CARL. *The Book of Fine Prints.* New York: Crown, 1937.

– –. *Prints: Thirteen illustrated essays on the art of the print selected for the Print Council of America by Carl Zigrosser.* New York: Holt, Rinehart and Winston, 1962.

Chapter Two: THE BITTEN

Methods

DEHN, ADOLF, and BARRETT, LAWRENCE. *How To Draw and Print Lithographs.* New York: Tudor, 1950.

HAYTER, S. W. *About Prints.* London: Oxford University Press, 1962.

–. *New Ways of Gravure.* New York: Pantheon, 1949.

HELLERS, JULES. *Printmaking Today.* New York: Holt, 1958.

HIND, ARTHUR MAYGER. *Guide to the Process and Schools of Engraving.* London: British Museum, 1933.

– – –. *History of Engraving and Etching.* Boston: Dover, 1927.

IVINS, W. M. JR. *How Prints Look.* Boston: Beacon, 1943.

PETERDI, GABOR. *Printmaking, Methods Old and New.* New York: Macmillan, 1959.

PENNELL, J. and E. R. *Lithograph and Lithographers.* London: 1898.

Chapter Three: LOVE AND DEATH

HIND, ARTHUR MAYGER. *The Master E. S., and the "Ars Moriendi".* Engraving during the fifteenth century.

– – –. *Andrea Mantegna and the Italian Pre-Raphaelite Engravers.* New York: Stokes, 1911.

– – –. *Early Italian Engraving.* 2 vols., New York: Knoedler, 1938-48.

– – –. *Introduction to a History of Woodcut.* 2 vols. Detailed survey of work done in the fifteenth century. Boston: 1935.

GEISBERG, MAX. *Martin Schongauer.* New York: Knoedler, 1928.

JOACHIM, HAROLD. *Prints: 1400-1800.* Minneapolis: Institute of Arts, 1956.

KRISTELLER, PAUL. *Engravings and Woodcuts by Jacopo de' Barbari.* New York: Wunderlich, 1896.

MONGAN, ELIZABETH and SCHNIEWIND, CARLO. *The First Century of Printmaking.* Chicago: Chicago Art Institute, 1941.

Chapter Four: DÜRER.

BRION, MARCEL. *Dürer: His Life and Work.* New York: Tudor, 1960.

HIND, ARTHUR MAYGER. *Dürer, His Engravings and Woodcuts.* New York: Stokes, 1911.

KURTH, WILLI (ed.). *Albrecht Dürer, Complete Woodcuts.* New York: Crown, 1946.

PANOFSKY, ERWIN. *Albrecht Dürer.* 2 vols. Princeton: Princeton University Press, 1943.

Chapter Five: AFTER DÜRER

CLARK, J. M. *Dance of Death by Hans Holbein.* London: Phaidon, 1947.

COLLINS, LEO C. *Hercules Seghers.* Chicago: University of Chicago Press, 1953.

Dance of Death, Holbein. London: 1916. Enlarged facsimiles.

DOBSON, AUSTIN. Introduction, *The Dance of Death by Hans Holbein.*

HIND, ARTHUR MAYGER. *Hans Holbein the Younger, The Dance of Death and other Woodcuts.* London: 1912.

MÜNZ, LUDWIG. *Breugel, The Drawings.* Greenwich, Conn.: Phaidon, 1961.

Chapter Six: REMBRANDT

HIND, ARTHUR MAYGER. *Rembrandt's Etchings.* London: Methuen, 1920. Catalogue.

MÜNZ, LUDWIG. *Rembrandt.* New York: Abrams, 1954.

– –. *Rembrandt's Etchings.* 2 vols., London: Phaidon, 1952.

VAN GELDER, J. G. Dutch Drawings and Prints. New York: Abrams, 1959.

Chapter Seven: CALLOT and PIRANESI

Callot

BECHTEL, EDWIN DE TURCK. *Jacques Callot.* New York: Braziller, 1955.

GREEN, J. H. *Jacques Callot.* London: J. Barfield, 1804.

Jacques Callot: Selected prints from collections of Rudolph L. Baumfield and Lessing J. Rosenwald. Washington: National Gallery of Art, 1963.

Piranesi

HIND, ARTHUR MAYGER. *Catalogue of Prisons and Views of Rome by Piranesi.* London: Cotswold Gallery, 1922.

HUXLEY, ALDOUS, and ADHEMAR, J. *Prisons.* 1949.

MAYOR, A. H. *Giovanni Battista Piranesi.* New York: Bittner, 1952.

Chapter Eight: HOGARTH

ANTAL, FREDERICK. *Hogarth.* New York: Basic Books, 1912.

BECKET, R. B. *Hogarth.* Hollywood, Fla.: Transatlantic, 1949.

DOBSON, AUSTIN. *William Hogarth.* London: 1907.

HIND, ARTHUR MAYGER. *William Hogarth, His Original Engravings and Etchings.* New York: Stokes, 1912.

HOGARTH, WILLIAM. *The Analysis of Beauty, 1753*. With plates, 1909.

QUENNELL, PETER. *Hogarth's Progress*. New York: Viking, 1955.

WALPOLE, GILPIN, LAMB, HOGARTH. *Anecdotes of William Hogarth*. 1833. Essays.

William Hogarth, Marriage à la Mode and other engravings. New York: Lear, 1947.

Chapter Nine: GOYA

FAURE, ELIE. *The Disasters of War*. Vienna: Phaidon, 1937.

HIND, ARTHUR MAYGER. *Francisco Goya*. New York: Stokes, 1911.

HUXLEY, ALDOUS. Foreword to *The Complete Etchings of Goya*. New York: Crown, 1943.

KLINGENDER, F. D. *Goya in the Democratic Tradition*. London: Sidgwick and Jackson, 1948.

Goya Drawings and Prints: From the Museo del Prado and the Museo Lazaro Galdiano, Madrid, and the Rosenwald Collection. Washington: National Gallery of Art, 1955.

Chapter Ten: DAUMIER

DELTEIL, LOYS. *Honoré Daumier*, 10 vols. Paris: 1925-29. Catalogue.

HAZARD, N. A., and DELTEIL, LOYS. *Daumier*. 1904. Catalogue.

LEMANN, BERNARD. *Introduction to Honoré Daumier*. New York: Reynal, 1946.

WARTMANN, WILHELM. *Honoré Daumier*. Zurich: Manesse Verlag Conzett & Huber.

Chapter Eleven: ROUAULT

COURTHION, PIERRE. *Georges Rouault*. New York: Abrams, 1962.

GETLEIN, FRANK and DOROTHY. *Georges Rouault's Miserere*. Milwaukee: Bruce, 1963.

SOBY, JAMES THRALL. *Georges Rouault*. New York: Museum of Modern Art, 1947.

VENTURI, LIONELLO. *Rouault*. Translated by JAMES EMMONS. Paris: Skira, 1959.

WHEELER, MONROE. *Introduction to Georges Rouault's Miserere*. New York: Museum of Modern Art, 1952.

Chapter Twelve: KÄTHE KOLLWITZ

BASKIN, LEONARD. *Käthe Kollwitz*. Northampton, Mass.: Smith College, 1958.

BITTNER, HERBERT. *Käthe Kollwitz Drawings*. New York: Yoseloff, 1959.

KLIPSTEIN, A. *The Grafic Work of Käthe Kollwitz*. 1955.

ZIGROSSER, CARL. *Käthe Kollwitz*. New York: Bittner, 1946.

– –. *Käthe Kollwitz*. New York: Braziller, 1951.

Chapter Thirteen: PRINTS AT PRESENT

American Prints Today. New York: Print Council of America, 1959
1962.

Associated American Artists Catalogues, New York.

Brooklyn Art Museum Catalogues.

BUCHHEIM, LOTHAR GÜNTHER. *The Grafic Art of German Expression*
ism. New York: Universe, 1960.

International Biennial of Prints. Cincinnati: Cincinnati Art Museum.
Catalogues.

CRAVEN, THOMAS. *A Treasury of American Prints.* New York: Simon
and Schuster, 1939.

JOHNSON, UNA E. *Ten Years of American Prints.* New York: The
Brooklyn Museum, 1956.

LIBRARY OF CONGRESS. *19 National Exhibitions of Prints.* Washington.
Catalogues.

MYERS, BERNARD S. *The German Expressionists.* New York: Praeger,
1956.

MURRELL, WILLIAM. *A History of American Grafic Humor, 1747-*
1938. 2 vols. New York, Praeger.

POPE, ANNEMARIE H. *Smithsonian Institution Traveling Exhibition*
Service Catalogues. Washington.

SACHS, PAUL. J. *Modern Prints and Drawings.* New York: Knopf,
1954.

SLOAN, JOHN. *Gist of Art.* New York: American Artists, 1939.

Tamarind Lithography Workshop Catalogues. Los Angeles.

ZIGROSSER, CARL. *Mauricio Lasansky.* New York: American Federation of Art, 1960.

– –. *Misch Kohn.* New York: American Federation of Art, 1961.